ABYSSINIAN STOP PRESS

FAREWELL IN ADDIS ABABA

ABYSSINIAN STOP PRESS

EDITED BY

LADISLAS FARAGO

Author of "Abyssinia on the Eve"

WITH CONTRIBUTIONS BY

PATRICK BALFOUR, EDMUND DEMAITRE,
MORTIMER DURAND, STUART EMENY,
LADISLAS FARAGO AND
MAJOR-GENERAL J. F. C. FULLER, C.B., C.B.E., D.S.O.

*Thirty-five Illustrations
from photographs*

London
ROBERT HALE & COMPANY
102 Great Russell Street W.C.1
MCMXXXVI

MADE AND PRINTED IN GREAT BRITAIN BY PURNELL AND SONS LTD
PAULTON(SOMERSET) AND LONDON

CONTENTS

PAGE

A SOLDIER-JOURNALIST IN ABYSSINIA
by Major-General J. F. C. Fuller, C.B., C.B.E., D.S.O.   11

FIASCO IN ADDIS ABABA
by Patrick Balfour   47

THE CRAZY WAR
by Mortimer Durand   81

WITH THE LIONS OF JUBA
by Edmund Demaitre   129

UNDER FIRE WITH THE EMPEROR
by Stuart Emeny   165

THE "BUSU TSHIKI-TSHIK"
by Ladislas Farago   201

SUPPLEMENT:
(*a*) THE WAR IN BRIEF   249
(*b*) SEVEN MONTHS OF WAR   250
(*c*) THE LEAGUE OF NATIONS AND THE ABYS-
SINIAN WAR   253

vii

LIST OF ILLUSTRATIONS

FACE PAGE

FAREWELL IN ADDIS ABABA . *Frontispiece*

MENELIK'S WAR-DRUM IN THE FIRE OF INTER-
NATIONAL PRESS-PHOTOGRAPHERS . . . 16

FATHER IS THE WARRIOR, BUT HIS SON CARRIES
THE EQUIPMENT 17

THE EMPEROR LEADING SOLDIERS TO BATTLE . 24

EACH ROOF HAS ITS OWN RED CROSS . . . 25

ITALIAN TANK AMONG CACTI 32

IN AN ABYSSINIAN CAMP 33

ABYSSINIANS LEARNING THE ROMAN SALUTE . 48

ITALIANS "ADVANCING" ON MAKALE . . . 49

OLD WARRIOR IN HIS SUNDAY BEST . . . 64

ABYSSINIAN CHILDREN PLAYING AT SOLDIERS . 65

ABYSSINIAN "FORT" 80

ITALIAN BOMBERS OVER AMBA-ALADJI . . . 81

FIELD WIRELESS—ABYSSINIAN STYLE . . . 96

FIRST POISON GAS—THEN DENTAL TREATMENT . 96

BEEF FOR THE FRONT LINE 97

NEWS-REEL CAMERA MORE INTERESTING THAN WAR 112

RED CROSS TENT AT DESSIE BLOWN UP BY ITALIAN
BOMB 113

AN ITALIAN BOMBER AND ITS ABYSSINIAN COUNTER-
PART 128

PRESS LORRY IN DIFFICULTIES 129

FRENZIED WARRIORS HEARING PROCLAMATION OF
WAR 144

FOOD FOR THE HYENAS 144

BRITISH RED CROSS TRUCK ON THE DESSIE ROAD 145

LIST OF ILLUSTRATIONS

FACE PAGE

WAR CORRESPONDENTS AT EASE 145

ITALIAN CONSUL OF GONDAR LEAVES ABYSSINIA . 160

ABYSSINIAN SAMARITANS 161

MAKALE AS THE ITALIAN AIRMEN SAW IT . . 176

ADOWA, UNCHANGED SINCE 1896 177

TINY ABYSSINIAN HUTS—POOR TARGETS FOR ITALIAN
BOMBS 192

STRANGE WARRIORS 193

MOBILISATION IN HARRAR 208

RAS GUGSA GOT A NEW UNIFORM . . . 209

ITALIAN ANTI-AIRCRAFT GUN—AGAINST WHAT? . 224

WOUNDED BELGIAN OFFICER AFTER BOMBING OF
DESSIE 225

A SOLDIER-JOURNALIST IN ABYSSINIA

By MAJOR-GENERAL J. F. C. FULLER
C.B., C.B.E, D.S.O.

*Military Correspondent to the "Daily Mail,"
with the Italian Army in North Abyssinia.*

A SOLDIER-JOURNALIST IN ABYSSINIA

My Outlook on the Approaching War

When, late last September, it was decided that I should go to Eritrea as Special Correspondent to the *Daily Mail*, though my information was of the meagrest I set about appreciating the military situation.

The first thing which struck me was the size of Abyssinia, and the second its strategical security. Topographically this country, nearly as large as France and Germany together, may be divided into three main areas, which I will call A, B and C. The first includes the whole land lying west of longitude 40°, and consists of a jumbled mass of mountains and valleys; the second covers Danakil and Aussa, north of the great Addis Ababa—Harar spur; and the third the Ogaden country south of it and abutting on Italian Somaliland. In these three areas the climate differs marked': in A it is temperate, in B unbearably hot and in C tropical in the south and temperate in the north. Generally speaking, water is scarce, except during the rains. In short, strategically, Abyssinia is like a porcupine bristling with quite exceptional difficulties.

What of its inhabitants, which number something between seven and ten millions? They comprise a jumbled mass of peoples and races, the political and social structure of which is shaped by three factors: religion, feudalism and slavery. The first is part Christian of a debased magical kind; part Mohammedan, and part pagan, and the second is of a loose, early medieval European order. The Negus, or Emperor, is King of the Kings, the Kings being represented by the Dedjacs, Rases, etc.; barons and chieftains who, possessing armed bands of their own, are frequently at war with each other and not infrequently at war with their overlord. From this it will be seen that the Abyssinian political system differs greatly from the Italian; for whilst both are autocratic, the first is very loosely and the second very firmly centralised.

Turning to resources, so important in war, whatever may be the undeveloped wealth of the country, the developed is limited by slavery on the one hand and lack of communications on the other. The first kills initiative, and combined with the feudal system establishes militarism as the sole pastime of the Rases. The second maintains the country in a state of chronic poverty which, when coupled with the military spirit, breeds cupidity among the Rases, a strategical factor which was made the most of by General Napier nearly seventy years ago.

Again, as the feudal levies are no more than loosely knit bands of armed men lacking in organisation and means of supply, in order to live they are reduced to foraging, which means either limited concentrations, temporary concentrations, or movements governed not by strategical requirements, but by economic needs.

Bearing this point in mind, it at once struck me that lack of communications was the Negus's greatest tactical asset; because, as his feudal bands possessed but the most rudimentary supply organisation, to them roads were nothing like so vital as to the Italians. Consequently, strange as it may seem, my opinion was that, from the Abyssinian point of view, the Addis Ababa—Jibuti railway and the Harar—Berbera road were strategically a disadvantage. True, they enabled supplies to enter the country; but, truer still, they presented the Italians with a real objective to strike at. Without the railway, Addis Ababa, though it might remain the capital, would be like any other town, but linked by it to outer civilisation it became a capital fixed. In consequence its cutting would not only be an economic set-back, but an overwhelming moral blow, because once cut the capital would be strangled, and once strangled the hub would be knocked out of the Negus's feudal wheel.

I next turned to a very important factor, namely the approaches through the three areas into which I had divided the theatre of war. First there is Napier's old track running from near Massawa, the Italian northern base of operations, southwards towards Dessye and thence to Addis Ababa; secondly, there is a track from Assab in southern Eritrea across the suffocating Danakil and Aussa provinces towards the railway, and thirdly, several towards this same objective from Italian Somaliland, of which the most likely appeared to me to be that of the Shibeli river north of Mogadishu. In order to relate them to the three main sub-divisions of the theatre of war, I will call them *a*, *b* and *c*.

Having completed this brief survey, and remembering that in weapon-power, means of transport and supply, the Italians were incalculably superior to the Abyssinians, it seemed to me that the war would take the following form: that the Italians would establish their base depôts at Massawa, Assab and Mogadishu, and simultaneously advance along all three approaches. Along *a* I expected to see an advance of mobile columns composed of Alpini regiments and units which had been put through if only a brief course of mountain warfare training; their object being not to occupy Addis Ababa, but to distract the enemy's attention and induce him to concentrate his main strength in country in which he felt he could fight more advantageously. The aim being to draw his fighting forces away from *b* and *c*.

Along *b* and *c* I expected to see highly motorised and mechanised columns strongly supported by aircraft pushing forward, their object being the railway. As regards column *b*, the distance it would have to traverse was some 300 miles, and for column *c* about 500. Therefore at an average advance of ten miles a day, I considered that the railway would be reached in about seven weeks. From there an advance could be made on Addis Ababa, a distance of 250 miles, and moving at the same average speed, this would take four weeks. In all this would mean roughly three months, or, say, four allowing for unseen contingencies. I did not consider this an impossible task, seeing that, in 1868, Napier had marched a similar distance, 758 miles, in about the same time.

It will be seen from this project that my opinions were exceedingly optimistic. I expected the war, should it begin in October (as it did) to end by February, that is to say its military phase. How long the pacification of the country, its police phase, would take I had no idea. So with this picture in my mind as a back ground to work upon, I set out from London to the seat of war on October 3.

Period of the Political Attack

I arrived in Massawa on October 17, having travelled in the same ship as did Marshal Badoglio, then on a visit to the front.

Though the roadstead is good, Massawa is a third-rate oriental port, dirty, fly-blown and dusty. In spite of it then being the middle of October it was sweltering hot, and what it must be like in mid-summer does not bear

MENELIK'S WAR-DRUM IN THE FIRE OF INTERNATIONAL PRESS-PHOTOGRAPHERS

Father is the Warrior, but his Son Carries the Equipment

thinking of. So far as I could see it was exceedingly ill provided for a great expedition. One long wharf without a single crane on it bordered its sea front; the town is nine-tenths native without a decent hotel or even a presentable saloon, and from it the communications leading southwards to Asmara are restricted to a metre gauge mountain railway and one fair yet exceedingly twisty motor road. Here I at once saw was the bottle-neck of the northern campaign. That on so slim a stem the Italians were later on able to hang an army of over 300,000 men certainly redounds to their credit.

From Massawa to Asmara, as the crow flies, is about forty-five miles, yet the rise in altitude is from sea level to well over 7,000 feet, and the change in temperature is from tropical to temperate. In fact, to those who can stand a somewhat rarified atmosphere, Asmara and most of Northern Abyssinia are a health resort, and this fact alone accounts for the slightness of sickness among the Italian troops.

Having some knowledge of mountain warfare and its needs, my first interest was the question of communications, because the supply of food and ammunition, however prosiac they may seem, is the foundation of strategy, as in its turn strategy is the foundation of tactics. But before I examine this subject I will sketch in very briefly the situation as it faced me on my arrival.

To begin with, Mussolini, from what he told me in Rome, wanted Abyssinia but he did not want a war, and failing an open-armed surrender on the part of the Negus, then the minimum of bloodshed, because his object was occupation and not plunder. He knew that the Rases were all at sixes and sevens, that revolt was latent, and he was still doubtful whether the League would be able to enforce sanctions. To gain his end the campaign opened far more as a political than as a military operation. Under General de Bono an Army of some 130,000 strong was assembled in Eritrea, not so much to break down opposition as to overawe the enemy by a show of force. These tactics were eminently successful, for the Mareb was crossed on October 2nd, northern Tigré was occupied, barely a shot having been fired, and by the 10th the line Aksum—Adowa—Entishu—Adigrat was secured. Then the inevitable happened, the weight of the Army in front set such a strain on the communications that, though supply did not actually break down, the advance had to be halted. Here I will turn to the question of roads.

From Asmara southwards run three main highways to Adowa, Entishu and Adigrat. They run through a country consisting of broad valleys cut up and separated by rugged mountains and a mixture of ambas (sugar-loaf hills) and South African kopjes and table-tops. Cultivation is sparse, aloes abound and so do cacti and thorn. In places there is jungle in others arid rock. At times the soil is brick red, at others white, but it is generally shaly and mud-coloured. The rock is easily pulverised into dust, which generally lies inches deep upon the roads. It is an ideal country for sharpshooter and machine gunner, and in places is well suited for tanks. For aircraft it is not so inviting, because landing grounds are few, and cover from air observation is universal.

The road I knew best, for I have travelled along it many times, is that leading from Asmara to Adigrat, and thence on to Dolo. It is well engineered and its first lap is comparatively easy going. Part of its surface is tarred, but from Sanganetti to Adigrat it resembles the teeth of a saw set into the side of the mountain ridges. How many hair-pin bends it contains I do not know, but in thirty-one miles of it there have been counted 1,700.

On such a road as this, and the other two are but a little less difficult, accidents were frequent. Not only were there many head-on collisions, but not a few lorries had the misfortune to run over the side. At one hair-pin bend I remember seeing four or five smashed to matchwood and lying in the valley a thousand feet below the spot from which they took their death plunge. How this actual accident happened was obvious: a lorry column had passed along, each machine throwing up a blinding cloud of dust; one had not seen the bend and had gone over and three or four others had followed it to destruction.

It certainly struck me so at the time and to-day I see no reason to revise my opinion, that General de Bono's basic problem was supply. Tactically there was nothing to stop him moving on Makale, and had he broken up his heavy Corps formations into three or four mobile columns of some 10,000 men each, and held the surplus in rear, the difficulties of supply would have been vastly reduced and the advance in proportion accelerated. But this would have meant a reversion of policy, for it would have substituted military for political action. Further, his men were in no way trained for mountain warfare, and except for his Native Corps, his troops were composed of Regular conscripts and Blackshirt Militia organised for war in Europe. Again, during this early period of the war, the Italian Higher Command was, I think, strongly inhibited by what may be called the "Adowa complex." In 1896 Italy had suffered one of the greatest disasters in the history of Colonial wars, and this disaster was very largely attributed to General Baratieri splitting his army into columns, for they were attacked in detail and almost annihilated. Were the Abyssinians to-day as good fighters as their predecessors of forty years ago? This was not yet known for there had been little or no fighting. As a matter of fact such a question did not arise, because, as this war was soon to show, the deciding factor was machine-power and not man-power, the machine gun alone having bereft the Adowa horde tactics of all value. Nevertheless, General de Bono can hardly be blamed for being cautious, for had the campaign opened with even a minor disaster, the effect on the political situation might well have been catastrophic.

Maintaining his army in three Corps masses, the right Corps at Adowa, the central at Entishu and the left at Adigrat, the improvement of communications went on apace; the mountain roads being continually widened, their gradients eased and their surfaces improved.

Meanwhile Marshal Badoglio, Mussolini's Chief of Staff, who had landed at Massawa on October 17th, made a complete tour of the front and the rear areas. It is possible that the pause after the occupation of Adowa—Adigrat had made the home Government anxious; but I am inclined to think that the now general talk of sanctions was forcing Mussolini to consider a more drastic policy of conquest. Thus far there had been practically no fighting, and yet Abyssinian chieftains were surrendering daily; but should the League go into alliance with the Negus, and this is what sanctions meant, a tremendous stimulant would be administered to his enemy, which by raising his morale would force Mussolini to substitute military conquest for political infiltration. Further, I am strongly of opinion that fear of sanctions persuaded General de Bono to push on with his advance before his communications were ready. My reason for this is that, on October 28th, I visited a considerable section of the front, and came to the conclusion that, though Makale could at any moment be occupied by a small mobile column, a general advance was unlikely, because it could not be adequately supplied. As a matter of fact I was wrong, because on November 3rd the next forward movement was initiated.

This advance was made by the left Corps leading, its objectives being Makale and Dolo, whilst the central and right Corps were held back in echelon. There being no fighting, the operation, in spite of an unexpected deluge of rain, was rapid, for Makale was peacefully occupied on November 8th.

Whilst during the move forward I had found the tracks abominable, on my return journey, on the 9th, I found them in many places impassable, except by pack animals and light cars. So once again it happened that the communications could not maintain the forward troops. The centre and right were held back and the position of the left Corps became precarious. Nevertheless, by the end of the month, troops, mainly friendly native bands, were pushed down to the Takkaze river, where they occupied the fords. Meanwhile the Tembien massif, which lies south of Adowa and west of the Adowa—Makale track, having never been cleared became a thorn in the side of the Italian main lines of communication. It was the home country of Ras Seyoum, who soon proved himself to be an able guerilla leader.

Such was the situation when, on November 18th, sanctions were imposed and the whole nature of the war was changed.

The Abyssinians assume the Offensive

In themselves the sanctions agreed upon at Geneva mattered very little, because the launching of the war itself had all but bereft the lire of its purchasing power. Yet from the point of view of the war their influence was decisive, for by stimulating the Negus they exasperated Mussolini. No longer was it now possible to rely on a slow penetration of the country; instead action was demanded even if of a ruthless kind; for were sanctions to be extended to oil, or were the Suez Canal to be closed, as was daily demanded in the British press, the war must collapse and with it in all likelihood the entire Fascist regime. In short, the economic blockade not only compelled Mussolini to fight for the conquest of Abyssinia but for his political existence in Italy.

His immediate answer was to recall de Bono, the politically-minded General and replace him by Marshal Badoglio the professionally-minded soldier, who landed at Massawa on November 28th and forthwith took over command.

The problem which faced him was as difficult as any Commander-in-Chief could be confronted with. He found an Army of some 200,000 men more or less distributed as a political demonstration on a front of about 300 miles with its rear communications incomplete and skirting the western and eastern margins of the Tembien massif. He also found himself faced by an enemy enthused by the League's action. If he withdrew his right wing, which was dangerously situated, he exposed himself to a *levée en masse* of the whole country south of him, for any sign of weakness on his part would have been taken immediate advantage of. Again, if he held on he risked local defeats, which would at once be magnified by the Abyssinians into major disasters. Further, it was obvious to him, for he told me so himself, that he could not advance until his communications had been greatly improved and large numbers of pack animals collected. Yet there can be little doubt that he there and then decided to turn the political attack into a great military offensive operation. Therefore, in order to cover his pause, which was destined

22

to last for over six weeks, he did two things: First he ordered the fortification of his front, and loose stone forts were constructed on every height and then linked together by machine gun posts. Secondly, he instituted so rigorous a press censorship that he drove ninety per cent. of the foreign journalists out of the country. Shortly after the war opened there were some seventy in Asmara, and by the middle of January less than ten.

Here I think he made a mistake. It is true that under General de Bono we journalists were given a very free hand. As it happened this fitted policy, for as the war was bloodless, we were for the most part reduced to reporting upon the pacific occupation of the country and such like subjects. Nevertheless, there can be little doubt that this generous treatment was from the Italian point of view reacting very favourably, for journalists readily responded to it, and in consequence world public opinion began to follow suit. Under Badoglio this policy was completely reversed, instructions being issued that no mention was to be made of the names of commanders, of localities and of units, and that on no account were movements of either Italian or Abyssinian forces to be referred to. The result was that journalist after journalist packed up and left, none too well disposed to the Italian cause. What the Marshal did not seem to realise was that it was of very great importance to him and his Government to weaken the League, and that the quickest way of doing so was to win over world opinion if only in part.

Having covered himself against attack and criticism, he set to work to prepare for a campaign, which was to be as ruthless as de Bono's had been considerate. First he ordered General Biroli, in command of the Native Corps, to clear the Tembien, where Ras Seyoum was causing considerable trouble. Secondly, he reversed the policy of allowing the civil inhabitants to retain their rifles, as it had been found that many of them were supporting that guerilla chieftain. Thirdly, he restricted the promiscuous bombing of Abyssinian columns and concentrations, because it was sound tactics to let the enemy mass. The one thing he very rightly feared was that they might cease to do so, might distribute themselves in small easily feedable groups throughout the country and start a guerilla war, for which the bulk of his army was ill-prepared. In fact, had he been faced by Pathan tactics, his army would have been in a most critical position.

From these actions it became clearly apparent to me that he was seeking battle on an extensive scale, and so convinced was I of this that, as early as December 5th, I wrote: "In spite of the meagreness of information during the last few days and perhaps on account of it, it would seem that the Tigrean air is becoming charged with electricity and that a storm is approaching. . . ." Thus far the Negus had been able to hold his northern Rases in hand; but from reports then being received from Addis Ababa it appeared that certain of them were straining at the leash, and that at any moment it might break. I then pointed out that on the Italian side the campaign had now reached a stage when it was no longer possible to advance in a Great Wall of China formation. I wrote:

"South of the rivers Takkaze and Gheva, without Herculean labours, it is no longer possible to advance three Corps of some 120,000 men in line; therefore a tactical turning-point has been reached. . . . To me it seems that a radical change is imperative and that it is possible that out of the present united advance of the Northern Army, two separate campaigns will be developed: one Corps operating towards Gondar and one on Amba

24

THE EMPEROR LEADING SOLDIERS TO BATTLE

EACH ROOF HAS ITS OWN RED CROSS

Alagi, whilst the third holds the Makale—Dolo position as a base for these Corps to operate from. This is the situation as I see it: The Negus, because of the lack of discipline among his Rases, is being pushed towards seeking a successful battle, and the Italians, because of the application of sanctions and changes in topography, are being forced away from what may be called 'overawing tactics' towards more normal operations of war. . . ."

I was given to understand that the Marshal expected an attack on his left flank. This I could not believe, because this flank was strongly fortified, and though as tacticians the Abyssinians are capable of almost any folly, I really could not see why they should run their heads against a brick wall when the greater part of their enemy's right flank lay open to them.

This flank rested on the Takkaze, and was, as I have described, held by detached posts, and was over-extended. Time and again I asked to visit this front, but was refused; for, from December 10th onwards all foreign journalists were literally interned in Asmara, not being even permitted to leave the precincts of that town.

Whilst this smoke cloud was being emitted, General Biroli cleared the Tembien; yet barely had he done so when a rumour reached the Press Office at Asmara that a considerable engagement had been fought on the Takkaze river near Mai Timchet; that the Abyssinian forces were under Ras Immiru, who had been reported advancing through the Province of Uoghera (north-east of Gondar) on December 5th. The next day we learned that he was in command of 3,000 warriors; that he had advanced in two columns and had forced an Italian detachment of about 1,000 strong back from the Takkaze, and had cut it to pieces in the pass of Dembeguina. Then, on the 19th, we were informed that the battle had opened on the 15th, was concluded on the 17th and that the casualties were as follows: more than 500 Abyssinians killed; Italian losses, 7 white officers and 20 white privates killed, also 48 native cadets and 197 native privates killed, the wounded being as follows: 2 white officers, 2 white privates and 25 natives. In other words 272 killed and 29 wounded which suggested massacre.

The result of this small engagement was extraordinary; for now that Marshal Badoglio had secured himself against press criticism, few things in actual fact could have been more advantageous to him, because his policy, in contradistinction to General de Bono's, was to seek and not to avoid battle. So long as his phalangial order held firm, battle was almost impossible; but now that it was broken, this set-back intoxicated the Abyssinians and filled them with an offensive ardour. As they poured into the Tembien, the whole of the Italian right wing had to be withdrawn to a little south of the Adowa—Aksum track, that is to the position it had held before the advance on Makale began. This resulted in the Italian front assuming the shape of the letter Z, and in consequence it was automatically split into two main groups, namely the Aksum—Adowa and the Makale—Dolo, connected by the Adowa—Makale, Entishu—Hausien and Adigrat—Dolo roads.

No sooner had the Abyssinians gained this small success than a force of 5,000 of them was reported to be massing in the neighbourhood of Abbi Addi and Enda Mariam Quarar in the Tembien, twenty-five miles west of Makale. There on the 22nd and 23rd a battle was fought between 7,000 Abyssinians and 4,000 Italians, the official casualties being as follows: Abyssinians, 700 killed and 2,000 wounded; Italians, 173 killed and 167 wounded. Again these casualties are irreconcilable with normal statistics; yet, as given, what they do show is, the extreme desire for battle on the part of the Italian Higher Command, not only in order to impress Geneva but to blood their own troops.

THE ITALIAN AND ABYSSINIAN TACTICS

Here I will pause in my narrative of the operations, and turn to the tactics of both sides; because, unless the reader has some slight knowledge of how each fought, it will be extremely difficult for him clearly to appreciate what follows.

First it must be realised that all soldiers, whether belonging to civilised or barbaric states, are closely circumscribed by tactical traditions. That is to say, they follow the technique developed during past successes rather than elaborate a new based on the powers of the weapons they are actually armed with. Like all other European armies, the Italian was saturated with what may be called the "bayonet tradition," whilst in their turn the Abyssinians were obsessed by the "spear tradition." Both are very similar, for both to prove effective demand masses of men, and yet in a mountainous country it is obvious that masses are suicidal when projectile throwing arms are used.

Now, from the very start of the war it should have been obvious to the Italian General Staff that the massing of the enemy was tactically the one thing to be desired, because the forces controlled by them being incomparably better equipped with projectile throwers—machine guns, cannon, tanks and aeroplanes, the more their enemy massed the greater would be his defeat. It is no exaggeration to suggest that a force of 5,000 Italians, so long as its men were trained for mountain warfare and well supplied, could almost in any circumstances easily defeat if not annihilate 50,000 Abyssinians. Equally important, it stands to reason that the smaller the forces used the more likely were the

Abyssinians to mass against them. In fact, their small-ness would be the bait and their weapon-power the hook hidden within it.

It was for this reason that, immediately after the out-break of the war, I could not understand why instead of advancing a number of mobile columns on a wide front, one great phalanx was used. I could not understand this because I did not then realise the political nature of the northern campaign, or that the troops employed in it were totally untrained for mountain warfare.

This lack of training not only forced the Italians to maintain a massed order of advance, but for a long time it detrimentally affected their air tactics; because, as the Abyssinians were totally unable to attack the masses, the Italian aircraft had to act independently; that is to say, without reference to ground action, to seek out the enemy masses and bomb them. This could and did result only in breaking up the enemy and at so great a distance from the front that no ground action could follow.

Quite early in the war this lack of co-ordination struck me forcibly, and I arrived at the following conclusions:

"Aircraft have two main functions, namely, reconnais-sance and attack, and as the Abyssinian air force is not worth considering, attack in this theatre of war is against targets and forces on the ground.

"The effectiveness of these two duties lies in inverse ratio to size of area and objective. Thus, the larger the theatre of war the more difficult becomes the first, and the smaller the target the more difficult is the second. Further, as regards the former, work is complicated by the fact that over half of Abyssinia is a mountainous country, in which the province of Tigré is entirely so; consequently this country offers few landing grounds, and the air reading of the ground is obviously more difficult among the mountains than on the plains. In such areas masses of men must be large to be seen. Also the indented nature of the ground enables them almost instantaneously to volatilise. They can scatter, hide and reassemble; in fact, during a week, the same force may be reported as a different force in half a dozen places, and in consequence completely confuse intelligence, and through intelligence planning. Personally, in such regions, I would put little trust in air reconnaissance unless it immediately preceded action or battle.

"Now as to attack. This problem centres round the question, when and where to strike at a target? And the answer is to be sought in examining three well-known factors, namely:

(1) "The marked effect of air bombing on concentrated human targets, such as men in mass or men retiring through a defile.

(2) "The insignificant effect of bombardment of large areas.

(3) "The demoralising effect of (1), and how rapidly human nature accommodates itself to (2).

"Therefore, I am of opinion that (2) should be sedulously avoided, and that (1) should be resorted to only when battle is imminent or engaged.

"With these facts in mind, I will turn to the operations in Tigré.

"As the reader will realise by now, the weakest link in the Negus's harness is the lack of an organised commissariat; consequently when his troops are concentrated, whole areas are devasted by foraging. Now, to let and even to encourage the enemy to waste his land, may be of the greatest tactical value; therefore indiscriminate bombing of every concentration shows a lack of tactical cunning. Personally, in a war like this one, a contest between organised and partially organised forces, so long as I commanded the former, I should welcome my enemy massing. Therefore, before a battle opened, I should allow very little bombing. I should look upon my aeroplanes as light and heavy cavalry, the duty of the first being reconnaissance and of the second the bombing charge.

"The light would go out to discover and report upon the enemy, and once discovered, in place of sending out the heavy to collect glory, I would hold them in hand. Next I would attempt to manœuvre my army in a way which would draw the enemy into an unsound tactical position, such as with his line of retreat running through a defile. Then I would egg him on; fall back and persuade him to mass his men. This done, I would stiffen up my front and hold him, and lastly launch on his rear my aerial charge. Once broken and compelled to retire, a pursuit of every available machine would be made."

I do not think that the Italian Higher Command fully appreciated these tactics, anyhow during the first three months of the war, and that it was not until the Abyssinians played into their hands they set them in motion. Even if this is so, it redounds to the wisdom of this Command's that eventually they put them into operation with such decisive effect.

Turning now to the Abyssinians, what do we see? An arrogant people whose easy victories of forty years before had endowed them with a fighting reputation which was not really theirs; or else a reputation which, under more modern conditions, they were unable to live up to. "Since 1895-1896," I wrote on November 23, "so I feel, the natural warriors of the hills and the plains have been contaminated by European military ideas, and are now more than less half-baked fighters. Though, as Regular armies go, the Emperor's professional army may be efficient, in my opinion it has weakened rather than strengthened his fighting power; because in such a country as this and with the people who inhabit it, true military power depends, not upon drillmastership, but upon planned irregular individual and band action.

"Should the Abyssinians wake up to the supreme fact that defence lies in the individual fighting man and not in the drilled mass, or for aught that in any mass, then woe to the Italian forces as at present trained and organised. Such of our own soldiers who have fought on the North-West frontier of India will understand this clearly: Picture an army of nearly a quarter of a million men, neither organised nor trained for this warfare, slowly creeping through a mountainous country many times the size of the Frontier, an army with communications stretching mile after mile in rear of it, and then introduce into this picture 50,000 Pathans split up into 200 fighting bands, always striking at weakness and never at strength, what will the success of that army be? . . .

"Fighting in their own country, their power to glean information is universal, for every fellow countryman and countrywoman is an ally. They know exactly where their enemy is, what he is doing, how he is situated, what he has got and what he lacks. Their handicap does not lie in their somewhat obsolete armament; because for the tactics which should be theirs, all they require is a good rifle and not necessarily a modern one, but in the deficiency of a supply organisation. In this respect they are so badly furnished that, instead of acting in independent groups . . . they mass in the fertile valleys and on the cultivated plains and so elaborate horde instead of group tactics. In either case they are come-and-go riflemen, and in consequence lack discipline and staying power."

With this picture in mind I will now return to the operations.

The Foundations of the Abyssinian Defeat

As I have hinted, the breaking of the Italian front on the Takkaze was a blessing in disguise. First it broke the phalangial order and forced Marshal Badoglio to think in terms of columns; secondly, it provided him with an excuse to tighten up his policy towards the civil inhabitants, many of whom had joined Ras Seyoum; thirdly, it intoxicated the Abyssinians into believing that they had their enemy on the run and that a second Adowa awaited their arms.

It is indeed strange how the shadow of this battle of forty years before influenced the strategy and tactics of this war. On both sides it induced the massing of men; on the Italian to prevent its recurrence and on the Abyssinian to effect it, and it was not until the latter had definitely proved that massing was a fatal mistake that the Italians began to shake their slow-moving phalanx out into self-contained mobile columns, which were far easier to supply, as their pack animals could subsist on local foraging.

Whether Marshal Badoglio had in his head a set scheme as to how he intended to conduct the war, I do not know; but what he did between his arrival and the middle of December leads one to suppose that he meant to carry on the advance in massed formations, striking the main blow with the left wing of his army.

During these six weeks the whole of his Z-shaped front was strongly fortified, and his left reinforced by a vast quantity of guns of all calibres from six-inch downwards. Meanwhile reinforcements were poured into Eritrea, the army being doubled in man-power. Above all things he wanted a big battle, and the fulfilment of this want depended not on him, but upon whether his enemy would commit the egregious blunder of attacking him in force. If they

ITALIAN TANK AMONG CACTI

IN AN ABYSSINIAN CAMP

did he knew that he could annihilate them; if they did not, then he was faced by a guerilla war, for which his army was neither organised nor trained, which might easily anchor him to his position for months.

Meanwhile Ras Seyoum and Ras Kassa, sheltered in the fastnesses of the Tembien, daily and nightly raided the Italian communications and actually crossed the Mareb and advanced to within rifle shot of Adi Quala. Lorries were shot up, posts cut to pieces and the communications thoroughly terrorised. So nervous did the Italian rear services become that from Christmas onwards nightly shots were heard in Asmara and several unfortunate civilian natives were killed by nervous sentries and road patrols. All the Abyssinians had now to do was to augment these guerilla exploits. At any time they could have overrun Western Eritrea and spread panic as far as Tesseney and Barentu. They did nothing of the sort. Instead, each minor success raised their conceit and brought them nearer and nearer to the brink of disaster.

During the first fortnight in the new year both sides were rapidly increasing in numbers, and, as we now know, both were preparing for battle: the Italian to free their communications, and the Abyssinian, so it would seem, merely to show off their prowess. When the clash came, as it did on January 19, it is not possible to say what actually happened; for according to Marshal Badoglio's *communiqué* it was a complete victory. He says: that whilst Ras Kassa and Ras Seyoum, based on the Southern Tembien, were preparing to attack the Italian "lines of operation" between Makale and Hauzien, they were attacked by the Third Army Corps and halted. Then, on the 22nd, the 2nd Blackshirt Division held up the enemy's main body near Abbi Addi and defeated it on the following day. During this fighting it was claimed that over 5,000 Abyssinians were killed, whilst the Italian losses in killed and wounded numbered 743. On the other hand, according to the *communiqué* issued by the Negus, though the Italians opened the attack their army was driven back and "pursued to destruction." He claimed as booty 29 guns, 175 machine guns and 2,654 rifles, as well as convoys of ammunition, mules and many prisoners.

Though at present no definite conclusion can be arrived at, it would appear that this battle was a drawn one, and for the following reasons: First, the Tembien was not cleared; secondly, the journalists on their way from Asmara to the front, were, on arriving at Adigrat, suddenly turned back as the country was not safe for them to proceed through; thirdly, the Abyssinian killed, unless whole groups were massacred in cold blood, is obviously a political figure. Five thousand killed means at least 25,000 wounded, that is 30,000 in all, omitting prisoners and missing, or half the British casualties on the first day of the Battle of the Somme. As in battles, even of the most desperate kind, casualties seldom exceed 20 per cent. of effectives, 30,000 means that the total Abyssinian forces in this battle must have numbered some 150,000 men. Such figures for the Tembien are simply fantastic, for this district had been foraged over again and again.

Meanwhile an extremely interesting operation had taken place in Italian Somaliland. It will be remembered that, when the war opened, my opinion was that the main operations should have been directed against the railway and not southwards through Tigré. And now that the war appears to be approaching its end, I see no reason to change this opinion. What prevented it seems to have been that from the start General Graziani's operation was looked upon entirely as a subsidiary one; that the climate did not allow of a concentration of European troops, and that the supply of native troops was limited and none too reliable. Further, Mogadishu was an indifferent post for a large army, and the communications leading north of it towards Harar were long and difficult to protect.

I remember quite early in the war thinking out this problem, and though I had few facts to guide me, I came to the conclusion that in Ogaden as in Tigré the fundamental problem was the maintenance and protection of communications. As the main line of advance roughly followed the Shibeli river, and as its right flank was fairly well covered by British Somaliland, any threat to the communications was obviously more likely to come from the west than from the east. I, therefore, expected to see a flanking force based on Dolo and Jet operating northwards to threaten the right flank of any Abyssinian forces attempting to cut Graziani's communications. Also I expected him to run a block-house line along the western margin of his Shibeli line of advance, which would have afforded it strong local protection. What he did and how his forces were organised and distributed I have no idea; for all I know is that early in the war he occupied Gorrahai, and that, on my return from Makale, on November 10, I heard that he had advanced to Daggabur. A few days later I learned that this was but one of his famous Lybian tip-and-run operations—a raid which, so far as I could see, was of no strategic value.

Nothing further was heard of him, when suddenly, on January 12, a great Italian victory was reported nearby Dolo on the Juba river, some 400 miles south of Harar and close to the Kenya border. There, on the 12th and the succeeding days, Ras Desta was heavily defeated in a battle called after an affluent of the Juba—Ganale-Doria, and driven in rout beyond Negelli. As it had now become normal procedure in the Italian official *communiqués*

5,000 Abyssinians were stated to have been killed, another 5,000 being added to this figure on the 27th.

This battle was an exceedingly important one; yet its true meaning escaped public notice, and certainly was not appreciated by the Negus. For over three months General Graziani had been toiling with his Harar operation, now he and presumably a considerable part of his main army had been pulled several hundred miles in the opposite direction; consequently, though he had gained a tactical victory he had simultaneously suffered a severe strategical defeat.

As I have pointed out, ever since the opening of the war his objectives had been Harar, the Jibuti railway and the Berbera road; now for weeks he would be forced to abandon them. Obviously what had happened was this: it was not so much the rains that had held him up as the persistent Abyssinian threat against the southern flank of his lines of communication, and to clear these he had been compelled to move south. Put slightly differently, as the northern political campaign under General de Bono had been disrupted by the economic blockade, the southern had been upset by a somewhat similar manœuvre.

The situation the Negus now found himself in was by no means a desperate one. In the north, though his Rases had attempted a large scale attack, they had gained some success and were still masters of the Tembien. All they need do now was to restart their guerilla war, and avoiding pitched battles aim their attacks at their enemy's lines of communication. In the south, though Ras Desta's army had been scattered, strategically Graziani was faced by a dilemma: either he could follow up his enemy or abandon the advance and return to the Harar operation. As a matter of fact, on account of the nature of the country northwards of Negelli and the difficulty of protecting his new line of advance, strategy dictated that he should turn towards Harar, and to restart his initial operation would take him several weeks.

Partially bunkered in the north and delayed in the south, it seemed, certainly to myself, that the Italian hope of finishing the military phase of the war before the monsoon broke in June was a slim one. Yet in war it is the unexpected which so often happens, and as I will now show the insensate foolishness of the Negus and his Rases presented victory to their enemy.

The Period of Decisive Battles

Whilst Marshal Badoglio was preparing for a set-piece battle, Ras Mulugeta, the Negus's leading general, at the head of an army which had in greater part been trained and equipped on European lines, in place of breaking away and extending the guerilla war, perpetrated the egregious blunder of massing against Makale and so offering his opponent a target to strike at. This was to play directly into the Marshal's hands; for had he not done so the vast preparations made would have been completely wasted.

Leaving him alone and fully realising that if he could destroy the Negus, who had now established his Headquarters at Dessye, he would knock the hub out of the Abyssinian wheel, the Marshal concentrated his bombing attack on that place as well as on the rear of his immediate enemy. Then, suddenly, on February 11, completely surprising the incompetent Mulugeta, he struck at him in the area which lies south of Shelikot and north of Antalo. This engagement, which lasted until the 16th and became known as the battle of Amba-Aradam or Enderta, was decisive in that it forced a general retirement through narrow defiles, and so presented to the Italian air force an ideal target to strike at. During it no less than 174 tons of bombs were dropped on the shattered horde, which was driven southwards in panic. In this battle the Italian casualties were 188 killed and 599 wounded, which are probably correct, the Abyssinian's being reported to be 5,000 killed as usual.

Whilst the broken enemy was being pursued, the Italian left wing advanced some twenty miles south of Amba Aradam and occupied Gaela, which lies on the Abbi Addi—Sokota track. Whereupon Ras Seyoum and Ras Kassa, in place of withdrawing westward, for this occupation threatened their southern line of retreat, committed the folly of moving eastwards. Once again this was to play into Italian hands, for the advance southwards on Amba Alagi could not without considerable risks be made until the Tembien was cleared, and had these two Rases moved westwards it would have been most difficult to do so. Realising the mistake his enemy had made, Marshal Badoglio at once pushed on to Amba Alagi, which he peacefully occupied on February 28. Simultaneously he advanced on Abbi Addi, one column moving against it southwards from the Abaro pass and another northwards from Gaela. There, on the 27th, he attacked them, almost completely hemming them in with his gun-fire. The result was the defeat of his enemy. Concerning this battle he commented in his *communiqué* : "The enemy has suffered such a defeat as to have lost any readiness to fight—a thing unheard of in the military history of Abyssinia." The truth is that mainly on account of air attack the Abyssinian morale was fast being destroyed.

No sooner was this battle ended than two Italian columns, again one moving from the north and the other from the south, struck at Ras Immiru, reported to be in command of 25,000 warriors. From near Dembeguina he was driven in rout towards the Takkaze. In this battle, as in its predecessors, air bombarding and machine gunning were so intense that the enemy's forces were fragmented and lost all cohesion.

At the time I was interested to learn that during these battles an increasing use was made of mustard gas. Not to terrorise the villages or directly to inflict casualties; but, instead, in order to protect the flanks of the columns as they advanced through the defiles of the Tembien. In other words, to shield them from guerilla attack. Though this is not mentioned in the Italian reports, the following extract from one of Marshal Badoglio's *communiqués* shows how rapidly weapon-power was influencing traditional tactics:

"For the first time in colonial military history numerous large units have been set in motion simultaneously with impressive masses of mechanised artillery of small and medium calibre and of light tanks, while the sky has been crossed by swarms of aeroplanes. All these complex movements have been regularly carried out, overcoming difficulties which might have seemed insuperable. The Third Corps moved into the Gaela zone across rugged and difficult ground, constructing as the march proceeded a motor track fifty miles long. Daily there were transported thousands of tons of material of all kinds, and supplies were twice carried by air for an entire army corps. Several groups of artillery of medium calibre, drawn by heavy tractors, covered over 300 miles, making daily stages of ninety miles, in part over tracks made during the action. From Massawa to the zone of operations 1,500 mules were carried by motor transport in two days alone. For communications during the battle over 800 wireless stations were set up."

The truth is, as I have said, machine-power was now daily compelling the breaking up of the original phalangial order into mobile columns, and that dearth of training in the protective duties of mountain warfare was more than made good by the use of mustard gas. In place of the laborious process of picketing the heights, the heights sprayed with gas were rendered unoccupiable by the enemy, save at the gravest risk. It was an exceedingly cunning use of this chemical.

Considering the nature of the country and the immense difficulties in supplying either concentrated or scattered forces of men, the shaking out into column formation was accomplished with remarkable rapidity; for on March 7 all columns were on the move: the left, composed of the First and the Native Corps, towards Amba Alagi; the Third from Gaela towards Fenaro; the Second on the Aksum-Gondar track; whilst a detached force was advancing from Om Ager on the Sudan frontier towards Noggara. Meanwhile the Fourth Corps began occupying the Semien mountains, several of their peaks rising over 14,000 feet.

As these movements were taking place, in the south General Graziani recommenced his activities against Harar: Jijiga was bombed again and again, and on the 29th, after due warning, the greater part of Harar was reduced to ashes.

The last day in March and the first two days in April witnessed the most astonishing events, the first of which was in its way decisive.

The Negus, be it remembered, was not only the head of his government, but was the government itself. It was for this reason that, for several weeks now, Italian aircraft had been hunting him in order to knock the hub, as I have called it, out of the Abyssinian wheel. So long as he remained alive, or his prestige held firm, there was every reason to expect that the war would continue: consequently it was of vital importance to him to maintain his prestige. Yet this is what he now failed to do, and in a way which was to prove suicidal.

Greatly perturbed by the Italian victories, he moved his Headquarters to Kworam, and from there, at the head of his small regular army supported by the fragments of the forces of Ras Kassa and Ras Seyoum, on March 31 he launched an attack on the head of the Italian left wing at Mia Chio. Supporting his troops by artillery and trench mortar fire, at first he seems to have gained some minor successes. Then the inevitable happened, held and decimated in front by shell and machine-gun fire, he was counter-attacked by aircraft, seventy machines dropping thirteen tons of bombs upon his men. Pulverised by high explosives, they broke back, were followed up, and, on April 3, were completely scattered in the battle of Lake Ashangi, where the now disorganized masses were bombed and machine-gunned by 140 aeroplanes. In this battle the Italians claimed that their opponent suffered 20,000 casualties of which 7,000 were numbered among the killed.

Simultaneously with this victory came the news that an Italian motorised column had advanced from Assab on the Red Sea, and after a march of sixteen days across 220 miles of the Danakil desert had occupied Sardo. Bombing machines were supplying it and further still were being used as troop carriers, conveying eight armed men on each flight. Meanwhile a somewhat similarly organised column, some 3,000 strong, was detached from the Second Corps, and in twelve days it advanced 186 miles and occupied Gondar.

These two remarkable operations, coupled with the victories of Mia Chio and Lake Ashangi, bring the period of decisive manœuvres and battles to an end. The stage was now set for the final scene, the advance on the Addis Ababa—Jibuti railway.

ABYSSINIAN STOP PRESS

The Advance on Addis Ababa and Harar

Always bearing in mind the nature of the country, the war now enters what I believe will eventually be considered to be its most remarkable phase. Difficult as it has always been to win battles in a mountainous region, hitherto rapid pursuits in such have been far more difficult still. Yet in this war the reverse is to be seen, battles are overwhelming and pursuits speedy beyond belief. The reason for this is two-fold: first, because the Abyssinians substituted mass tactics for guerilla warfare, and secondly because air attack and pursuit are almost as easy in a mountainous area as over desert or plain land.

First, it was the folly of the Abyssinian tactics which rendered the Italian victories possible, by offering targets to air attack. Secondly, it was aircraft which rendered pursuit effective, and how effective may be judged from one small incident, namely, a propaganda flight on April 14th of twenty-two Italian machines to Addis Ababa and back; when in seven hours they covered 700 miles. Compare this to the power of cavalry in the past. Even in open country, let alone roadless and mountainous, pursuits have seldom exceeded twenty-five miles in twenty-four hours, and then have generally petered out in a few days. In this war there is nothing to prevent them being continuous, and 700 miles in seven hours compared to twenty-five in twenty-four is a difference of 100 to one. In other words, aircraft have speeded up the pursuit 100 times. Thirdly, it was man-power which rendered the maintenance of the pursuit possible, man-power in administrative and not in combatant form. On the date just mentioned, Marshal Badoglio reported that in the northern theatre of war he was employing 170,000 men on the roads, and of these, 120,000 were soldiers. As the front was thinned out and the rear was thickened up with men, the more speedy became the advance; because, though the aeroplane opened the way, it was the lorry which supplied it, consequently the lorry was the basic factor in the pursuit.

For a moment I will turn to it during the fortnight following the victory of Lake Ashangi. On April 5 Kworam was entered under cover of sixty-four tons of bombs. On the 6th the advance was pushed on to Alomato, and two days later the road south was opened as far as Mia Chio. On the 10th Kobbo was sighted and on the 12th entered, the leading troops being supplied by aircraft. This day the Galla tribesmen joined hands with the Italians and Marshal Badoglio issued his proclamation abolishing slavery. Then, on the 15th, Dessye was occupied, a pursuit of 120 miles having been accomplished in nine days. Meanwhile, on the 13th, lake Tana was reached by the leading troops of the Second Corps; the Abyssinian customs post opposite Gallabat in the Sudan was occupied by a motorised and mechanised column, and, the day following, troops of the Third Corps reached mount Abuna Josef on the Socota-Magdala track. Without fear of contradiction, I think it may be said that nothing like this pursuit has ever before been witnessed in mountain warfare.

Of these several advances that on Dessye was the more spectacular. During it its van did not consist of motorised forces, as the ground was impracticable for vehicles. Instead, the Native Corps, also called the Eritrean Army Corps, 20,000 strong, was advanced from Kworam on April 9, and during its six days' march of 120 miles it was entirely provisioned by squadrons of aeroplanes. It was followed by a supply column of over 9,000 mules and camels, also partially provisioned by air, 120 tons being dropped, in rear of which tens of thousands of men were working on the roads. The combination of supply aircraft, pack animals and lorries was the foundation of this advance, and tactically the terror already caused by mustard gas undoubtedly speeded it up. With reference to the use of this chemical, a correspondent wrote on April 16: "Even more effective were the measures taken by the Italian Command to meet the Ethiopian tactics of taking cover in woods and bush in order to attack the Italian flanks and communications. Whenever possible the cover was impregnated with mustard-gas by bombing or shelling, and the unfortunate Ethiopians soon began to suffer terribly from gas burns. The loss of life was apparently small, but such large numbers were crippled or put into terrible pain that the morale of the army gave way. All thought of guerilla warfare was abandoned, and a general panic followed."

With the occupation of Dessye it is of interest to pause and look at the general situation of the various Italian columns. They take the form of an immense semi-circle, stretching from Gallabat to lake Tana, to Abuna Josef, to Dessye, to Sardo, to Gabridihari (south of Sassa Baneh), to Imi and finally to the upper reaches of the Ganale Doria. That is, as the crow flies, a semi-circle of no less than 1,300 miles in extent. Accepting 200 to 250 miles as the average radius of action of the Italian bombing machines, then from this semi-circle, except for the extreme west of Abyssinia, any portion of the country still unoccupied falls within the area of air bombardment, which as the columns contract on the centre can become more and more intense. What does this really mean? Not the economic blockade of the inhabitants and forces within it, but their moral blockade—the starvation of their nerve-power. Looked at slightly differently, each column of troops, whether motorised or not, is little more than a base for air action; as it were the protective guards of a series of aerodromes, the forward movement of which depends upon the speed at which the ground forces can manœuvre. In other words, if the aerodromes are compared to cannon and their aeroplanes to flying shells, then the troops on the ground are nothing more than an escort to the guns.

Bearing this picture in mind, the reader will at once realise the importance of Harar. Outside any question of it being the second city in Abyssinia and the Negus's natal town, in the present encirclement, the weak link in the semi-circle lies between Sardo and General Graziani's forces south of Sassa Baneh. This is undoubtedly one reason why, as I am writing, the advance on Harar is being vigorously pushed.

Here, Graziani, a general of considerable repute, seems to have had to face greater difficulties than the generals of the northern columns. Not only is the climate nothing like so favourable, but on account of the rains his advance has been time and again impeded. All said and done, mountains are made of rock; consequently, once a road is hewn, the rain will not affect it in the same degree as roads built in the plain lands. Though Graziani has been employing 30,000 men on road work, his progress has been slow, because stone has frequently to be transported many miles. In spite of this difficulty and the bushland which makes air observation in places impossible, on April 14 he attacked his enemy on the Giana Gobo, an affluent of the Fafan river, lying sixty miles west of Gabridihari. There he fought a battle on the 15th, 16th and 17th, and by flank attacks "constantly supported by waves of aeroplanes" broke up the Abyssinian forces, killing as he reported

3,000 men. As I write, he is closing on Sassa Baneh and Badoglio's advance from Dessye on Addis Ababa has begun.

How this war will end it is impossible to say; but there can be little doubt that, long before these words appear in print, Addis Ababa, Harar and Diredawa on the railway will be occupied. What will happen then is on the lap of the gods, and whether the war is to continue, collapse or enter a police phase must be decided by these occult powers. Yet, whatever takes place, this war will be looked back upon as one of the most remarkable ever fought. Not only does it show beyond dispute the enormous influence of modern weapon-power in such undertakings, but also it demonstrates clearly enough the changing nature of war between civilised nations. It is true that, in such wars, armaments are far more equal; yet it is also true that in them aircraft targets are far more abundant, because the population is more dense. If it is possible by means of chemical and high explosive bombs to demoralise the tribesmen of a mountainous region, how much more possible is it to demoralise the inhabitants in the overcrowded cities and industrial areas of the great civilised powers. Again, it may well be asked, what place have the old arms in battle when confronted by the new? Had the Negus been supported by a vast army of European cavalry, infantry and horse-drawn artillery, would he have been much better off? In many ways he would have been far worse off; because he would have had more mouths to feed and the air targets would have grown larger. What does this then lead us to suppose? That in another European war the decisive weapon will be the aeroplane, and when it has defeated or mastered its like, the masses below are at its mercy, and that the larger they are not only the more vulnerable will they become, but the greater will be the social upheaval following their catastrope.

FIASCO IN ADDIS ABABA

By PATRICK BALFOUR

*War-Correspondent to the "Evening Standard,"
with the Abyssinian Army in Addis Ababa and
Harar.*

ABYSSINIANS LEARNING THE ROMAN SALUTE

ITALIANS "ADVANCING" ON MAKALE

FIASCO IN ADDIS ABABA

I

USUALLY you get dysentery on the way up. Parched by the sand and the heat and the early morning start you shovel far too much ice (bad ice) into your mineral water from your large Japanese thermos; and when you stop at a station for food (Greek food: too much food) they shovel a lot more into your beer (Abyssinian beer). So you usually get dysentery.

But I was lucky. I only had my passport stolen. It was stolen at Diredawa, by one of the yattering Abyssinian mob in the Customs House, while I was trying to restrain the Abyssinian customs officer from rifling my suitcase entirely. One of the mob took it out of my pocket, and I never saw it again.

The journey is boring, but not too uncomfortable. The train is only a little less comfortable than a second-class carriage in France. But it is very slow. Sometimes the engine-driver has a row with the Greek who keeps one of the station restaurants and goes off without the first-class passengers while they are at lunch; they have to wait until he is ordered back from the next station. Sometimes the line is washed away by the rains; but they do not take long to repair it. Often you stop while somebody repairs the telegraph wire. You have interminable waits at the stations: stations bordered by cemeteries where men are buried who helped to build the line. The Greek pubs where you spend the nights have innumerable lean cats and pretty gardens of jasmine and vines. The beds are clean and hard and the cats jump on you through the mosquito-netting while you are asleep.

The country is dreary. First it is desert. Then it is drearier still: country of scrub and camel-thorn which is dreary because much of it could be cultivated and is not. There are monkeys among the camel-thorn. There are Danakils, lithe and wiry and wild, with spears. At the stations there are Abyssinians: guards of policemen with rifles, and that yattering mob, listless but noisy. They are not naked, like the more graceful Danakils, but dressed in dirty white to show that they are Christians and more civilized. The men carry out-of-date rifles and belts with cartridges which do not fit them, and their hair is fuzzy, like a golliwog's. The women look much the same, in their dirty white garments, but sometimes their hair is more picturesque, like a halo of fuzz. They are greasy, and smell of rancid butter. Their expressions, men and women, are hard. There is no gleam of sympathy in their eyes and they are too suspicious to smile.

It is hot, until the evening of the third day, when the train climbs steeply up to Addis and it is cold. When you get out on to the platform it is cold and damp, like Scotland, and you change quickly from your shorts into a thick tweed suit or breeches.

The climate of Addis is not tropical. Provided your heart will stand the altitude, it is not disagreeable in the dry season. In the daytime it is bright and sunny, at night it is cold.

Addis looks like a middle-western town but is built on hills. Also it is dense with eucalyptus trees: thin, scraggy ones, millions of them, ordered from Australia by Menelik, when he made it his capital, because there were no trees there at all and these grew quickly. Their smell is sweet but you get very tired of it, mixed with the reek of smoke from the native mud huts. The native huts are round and thatched with straw, and they are scattered anyhow among the eucalyptus groves. There is a native market and bazaar at one end of the town. Then there is the European town, like the Middle West: wide, untidy streets of shops, in no style of architecture, with corrugated iron roofs. Only the centre of the street was metalled for motor traffic. The population walked in the broad, stony gutters at the side, and the police, barefoot, in untidy blue uniforms, belaboured the population with rhinoceros whips, driving them into the gutters since, under a recent edict, they were not allowed to walk in the middle. The police wore belts full of cartridges, but only used whips. (The Secret Police were easiest to recognize, as they wore bright blue bands on their caps.)

The traffic was mixed: luxurious, expensive American taxicabs of the latest make, cavalcades of mules; a minor chief, perched pompously on his tiny mule, with armed retainers running after him; a string of coolies with sofas, bedsteads, packing-cases and grandfather clocks on their backs. (House-moving was cheap and easy in Abyssinia, where there were no pantechnicons: you could do it in an hour.)

The shops were plentiful and good, for Addis was always a European town; you could buy anything within reason, far more than in Djibouti. They belonged to Armenians and Greeks and Indians. There was a first-class grocery store called Ghanotakis, the Fortnum & Mason of Addis Ababa. But Ghanotakis had to go when the war started, as he was a Greek who had become an Italian through living in the Dodecanese. So his shop, with all its delicacies, was shut, and we got no more caviar. It was rumoured that the French Minister had the key, but that didn't help us.

The biggest store was Mohamedally's, where you could buy anything from a bicycle to a Seidlitz powder. Messrs. G. M. Mohamedally & Co. were the biggest traders in Abyssinia. They had branches all over the country, and each was run by an Indian (or two, or three, according to its importance), all called Mohamedally, all in golden turbans, all exactly alike. Mohamedally's at Jijiga was also a European guesthouse, and a nice Mohamedally greeted every arriving guest with the words "Good night. How you getting on?" When it was bombed in March Mohamedally's was flying the White Ensign. (The Admiralty took considerable umbrage at the report.)

There were French hairdressers' shops, and stationers' shops, where you could get all the European papers once a week, and pastrycooks' shops, where you ate cakes and drank coffee in the mornings.

There was a shop where a Russian Prince sold skins: monkey rugs and leopard rugs and black panthers' and lions' manes; and vodka, which he made on the premises. He tantalised us with rumours that Addis was shortly to have a night-club with ladies from Alexandria dancing among leopard skins; but it was one of those Russian dreams which never materialised. The ladies must have got held up indefinitely in the customs.

On one of Addis Ababa's hills was the cathedral, on another the old palace, on another the new. Square triumphal arches, still surviving from the Coronation though made, apparently, of cardboard, honoured the avenues which lead to the cathedral and the old palace. The Emperor lived in the new palace and transacted affairs of state in the old: a conglomeration of glorified sheds, open to the people, where hundreds of listless suppliants waited about all day in the dust but rarely got his ear. Here, on State occasions, the Emperor entertained his barons and their armies to banquets of raw meat and tej, the potent native drink, made of fermented honey, on which Abyssinians get drunk all over the country. (In some parts empty bottles, to put the tej in, are currency, while dollars are not.) On these days you saw hundreds of bleeding, freshly-killed carcases being carried up to the palace for the banquet, and afterwards the warriors, with the blood of the meat still fresh on their lips, rolled tipsily and arrogantly through the streets, the barons swaying on their mules, their lions' manes awry.

The new palace was built of grey concrete, in the style of a modern Swiss office block. Inside it was decorated by Messrs. Waring & Gillow, who were instructed to make it as much like an English country house as possible. (The Emperor had stayed in Norfolk with Lord Noel-Buxton, and had been much impressed.) It had dark panelling and red leather chairs and a certain comfort and dignity. It was to be finished for the reception of the Crown Prince of Sweden on his visit in January, 1935. He was due on the 9th, and the furnishings only arrived at Aden on December 27th. But with a hustle previously unknown in Abyssinia, they were rushed across the Red Sea, rushed up to Addis and rushed into place within twelve days. The last workman walked out of the back door as the Crown Prince walked in at the front.

Here the Emperor entertained us: once to a tea-party at which flunkeys in red and green served caviar sandwiches and champagne, once to an endless dinner during which the electric light failed five times.

The cathedral is a modern building, circular after the style of the Abyssinian Coptic Church. Services consist of monotonous chanting, with the priests facing the ikons and the congregation squatting on the floor round the outside aisle: women one side, men the other. Sometimes they go on all night, and you see the priests staggering out in the morning, exhausted and slightly drunk with the frenzy of their chanting and dancing. The vestments are tawdry: cheap foreign velvets and laces, spangles and tinsel and Woolworth jewellery. The ikons and wall-paintings are garish, only occasionally showing a trace of some Byzantine ancestry. Abyssinian painting is nursery poster-art, but often with a pleasant sense of design and composition to show what it might have become with some background of aesthetic tradition. But to the Amhara (unlike the Galla) art and craftsmanship are strangers. Abyssinia, as I saw it, has no architecture.

The pleasantest features of the city are the foreign Legations. They stand in ample compounds, outside the town, and their gardens (particularly the British) rival those of the Italian Riviera. The Legations were the centre of Addis's more reputable European social life. At the British Legation you read Shakespeare plays (largely in American) on Saturday nights and fished for sovereigns in the snapdragon on New Year's Eve. The French Minister gave large luncheons, which lasted till five o'clock. The German Minister gave agreeable dinners, and played Chopin to you afterwards, on the piano. The American Legation was unfurnished, and the Chargé d'Affaires lived in the Imperial Hotel. The Belgian Minister (the Doyen) was a grasswidower who had a very small staff and was reported to do all his typing himself. To the Italian Legation you went rather furtively, ate excellent food, refrained from commenting on the denuded state of the rooms (for everything was permanently packed in readiness for flight) and admired the challenge cups which the staff had carried off at the previous race-meeting (and which they carried off ultimately to Djibouti, so that the races in question could no longer be run). The Turkish Minister lived in a hotel until one day he remarked, ironically, that he had "left the Europe for Africa", and installed himself in an empty house, waiting for the furniture which his Government would not send until they saw how the situation was going to turn out.

When I arrived in Addis the rainy season had still six weeks to run. For three or four hours a day the rain beat like relentless machine-gun fire on the corrugated roofs. The gutters were morasses of yellow mud, the streams and rivers rushed in liverish torrents through the town, the open grass spaces were swamps and the countryside was impassable. The soaked hillsides were green, and perpetual cloud obscured the tops of the mountains. Everything was drenched in a Scotch mist. The green hillsides recalled Northern Italy: the lower slopes of the Alps in the winter rains. But, unlike Italy, they were sparsely cultivated. Here was rich land going to waste, under a people who preferred the sword to the plough. You could see in it a Promised Land for Italians: every speck of land cultivated with grain and fruit and vegetables, the hillsides terraced, perhaps for vines.

Its potential beauty sprang into being with the sudden end of the rains. The clouds lifted from the hilltops, the landscape lightened and, in a night, the meadows became a mass of yellow flowers. Then came the war.

Under a cloudless blue sky, with a vivid landscape falling away beneath it, the Emperor proclaimed general mobilization from the old palace: a somewhat staged mobilization, since most of the country was already, unofficially, mobilized. The order was read to a sea of black faces, while ravens wheeled ominously overhead in the blue sky. A great drum was beaten. The black faces broke into a pandemonium of war-cries. The correspondents stampeded to secure translations of the speech from the little Abyssinian Press Director who, in a morning coat, asked for silence for a further announcement in

55

vain. The correspondents clamoured for copies, that they might telegraph them at once to their papers. The little man was nearly swept off his feet and trampled underfoot by the correspondents. Finally he reached the sanctuary of the palace, clambered on to a gilt chair, and got silence for his announcement. It was of far graver import than the staged mobilization.

The Italians, that morning, had bombed Adowa.

II

The correspondents and other vultures, smelling war, began to arrive in Addis Ababa in June. By August they numbered fifty. By October, when the war started, they had topped the hundred. Before the exodus began in December over one hundred and fifty Press cards had been issued: yellow cards, decorated with the Lion of Judah and an unrecognisable Armenian photograph of yourself, which, in Amharic, requested whom it might concern to grant you every facility to move and photograph freely. Of course the freedom of circulation was a mockery, since it confined you to Addis Ababa, Harar, and the railway. But that is neither here nor there.

Each week a further trainload of journalists, cameramen, adventurers, arms touts, concession-hunters, mystery men, crooks, soldiers and doctors of fortune was spilt into Addis from Europe, Asia and America: the civilian Army which, from diverse motives, flocks from all over the world to the scene of a war. Some arrived without a penny in their pockets, hoping vainly for the best. Others arrived in style, with a prodigious quantity of luggage: mammoth medicine-chests, camping equipment, tin boxes full of tropical kit (which is not worn in Addis), cameras galore, motor-bicycles, even lorries. They thronged the streets on mule and horseback, in the expensive American taxicabs and even, occasionally, on foot (but not often, on account of "The Altitude", whose atmospheric qualities cover a multitude of laziness).

There were Englishmen, Frenchmen, quantities of Americans, Germans, Austrians, Poles, Swiss, Spaniards, Czechs, Soviet Russians, Dutchmen, Danes, Swedes, Egyptians, all but Italians, to add to the already polyglot nature of Addis Ababa's five thousand white (or off-white) inhabitants.

There was a Latvian Colonel with an eyeglass, in impeccable riding-costume on a fine white horse, who wore a variety of uniforms with rows of medals, who seemed familiar with the circus ring and who proudly flourished a certificate from the French Consul in Berlin to say that he had crossed the Sahara on a camel.

There was Colonel Haroun-al-Raschid ("H. al R." with a crown, was emblazoned on his luggage): a bald little Prussian who had instructed a Turkish machine-corps in the war and earned the title of King of Machine-guns (which apparently sounded enough like Haroun-al-Raschid to make no difference).

There was the persistent American lady who, when received by the Emperor, brought her own photographer to photograph them together, whom none of the Court officials could lure from His Majesty's side, on State occasions, and who wept (she said from religious emotion) when removed from the Empress's entourage where (with her photographer opposite) she had planted herself in Church.

There was a round-faced little Jap, cryptic and discreet, with a falsetto laugh, who sent endless cables to Tokyo, in Japanese (which none of the operators understood), stringing all the words together into one, to save money.

There was an excitable Spaniard in plus-fours on a

57

horse, who complained about the quality of the sherry, was always losing wads of notes, and wrote long messages home about the Catholics being behind the Government of Abyssinia. There was a Swedish big-game hunter with a wife like Greta Garbo. There was a Sudanese, like a monkey, with a Brazilian passport, who would skip up trees or crawl under the horses' hoofs to secure a good photograph. There was an airman from Cuba, an airman from Harlem, an airman from Monte Carlo. There was a Turkish general who was given command of an Army. And there were cameramen, faking glorious battle-films, living six in a room, developing their negatives at the wash-stand, and facetiously photographing one another in bed when there was nothing else to photograph.

The hotel proprietors began to rake in fortunes. They charged pension prices and provided uneatable food so that their clients were forced to eat elsewhere and pay for each meal twice over.

The principal hotel was the Imperial: a barrack-like structure run by a Greek. It overflowed into outhouses, where a nightwatchman kept you awake at night with a trumpet, until you gave him a dollar to stop. The lounge was bare like a station waiting-room. There was a notice-board and posters on the walls and a billiard table and barefooted Abyssinian waiters, serving drinks: gin and whisky and koniak (sic) and Abyssinian beer. At meals you drank Chianti; or so you thought, until, in a frenzy of anti-Italian enthusiasm on New Year's Eve, a group of correspondents took all the Italian Vermouth and Chianti bottles they could see and hurled them with imprecations from a first-floor balcony. The proprietor came out in a rage. "What for you do that? That Greek wine, not Italian." The Abyssinians were hardly more appreciative of this patriotic gesture. As a hard-drinking race, they thought it a wicked waste of good liquor, whether Greek or Italian.

The Europe Hotel was superior to the Imperial, but it was far from the centre of the town, so few correspondents lived there. You went there for a bath, as it had natural hot springs; or you went there to stand drinks to the mystery men, who usually preferred to conceal their mysteries in its more secluded surroundings. The mystery men were a problematical investment. You might come on a Rickett, and be rewarded, or you might come upon a considerable liability. All were invariably on the point of having an important interview with the Emperor, on the point of being put in command of an important Abyssinian unit, on the point of signing an important contract. But most of them remained on the point until the hotel proprietor struck and their Legations were forced to send them home third class, as depressed subjects.

After a time people got tired of the aggressive discomfort of the hotels and drifted away into flats and pensions, so that the proprietors were left high and dry. There was a pension run by the Emperor's Swiss chef, who gave the Emperor notice because he didn't get paid. There was a Swedish pension and a Russian pension. But the best, where I stayed during my two months in Addis, was the Deutsches Haus, run by a German couple from Tanganyika. It had a pleasant garden, full of sweet-peas, lilies, and chrysanthemums. Its food was German, not Greek, and included strawberries from an English Colonel's farm outside the town. Its only crab was a couple of anti-European geese, who if you were white, flew at you as you came up the path and pecked your boots.

The Deutsches Haus will always be associated in my mind with animals, since it was here that I helped to give an enema to a leopard. The leopard, still quite a child, belonged to the correspondent of the *New York Herald*, and had been suffering some time from a disordered inside. Having decided on the proper remedy, we collected all the strongest Abyssinians within reach to hold the animal down. But the leopard's reaction was unexpected. Clearly she mistook the operation for something else, for, far from resisting, she waved her legs in the air and purred and afterwards strutted around with adult pride. And her digestion remained impenitently obdurate.

Then there were the night-clubs: three of them, with cinemas combined. They showed old but high-class American talkies, translated into French, with a talking apparatus which deafened you. Each programme lasted at least four hours, as the machinery continually broke down and the audience trooped out to the bar while it was put right. The bars were quite up to Paris standards and prices. Whenever a proprietor thought his premises needed modernizing they were mysteriously destroyed by fire and reconstructed by the insurance companies at lavish expense. At Christmas the night-clubs became casinos, with a licence to run roulette tables for a month.

Round the army of journalists and adventurers grew an army of retainers. Each had his servant and interpreter, each his spies. Speaking the most curious versions of English and French were servants too well-educated to deign to brush your trousers, servants too ill-educated to be able to do so, servants who drank and servants who stank, interpreters from mission schools who read the Bible all day long instead of interpreting, interpreters who were medical students as well and continually left you in the lurch to attend an important surgical operation: all sorts of servants and interpreters.

I was fortunate in my servant. His name was Gabriel the Gift of Mary. I paid him half a crown a week, he brushed my trousers impeccably, and he only got drunk once a month. At Harar his outbreaks were rather more frequent, as he was able to get khat to chew, and khat is the Moslem substitute for alcohol. On these occasions, with his Homburg hat at a rakish angle and his robes awry, he would become obsessed with the idea that he was the Belgian Minister. But his shortcomings were few. So intent was he on saving me money that I had to sneak out by myself whenever I wanted to buy luxuries, and conceal them from him for fear of his parsimonious disapproval. I used to lie barefacedly when he asked me what I had paid for things, and often I had to go without necessities altogether because Gabriel the Gift of Mary found them too expensive for me and walked out of the shop. He used to deliver me long recitations on the respective cost of commodities in the various provinces of Abyssinia which he had visited, and Addis Ababa invariably came out dearest. On the other hand he was inconsistently prodigal in the purchase of flywhisks, of which I acquired a large and expensive collection.

My interpreter, like most Moslems, was called Hassan. He was a Somali, and had a supreme contempt for the Abyssinians, whose language he could not understand. For this reason he was rather a failure as an interpreter. Hassan had been sacked from the British Service in Somaliland for peculation. He was, indeed, the most avaricious man I ever met. Money obsessed him. In Addis Ababa he sold his blanket, his mattress, and every stitch of clothing he possessed, because prices were higher than in Somaliland and he would be able to refit his wardrobe cheaper on his return home. One night he was walking down a street of tej houses in Addis Ababa, with the ten dollars in his pocket which the wardrobe had fetched. A woman came out of one of the tej houses with a banknote, which she showed him, asking its value. Hassan saw a string of noughts, promptly said that the note was worth ten dollars, and paid her for it. Next morning he showed me what he said was a thousand dollar note. It was a 100,000 Rentenmark note of the inflation days after the war, a piece of wastepaper.

He went to the woman and demanded his ten dollars back. But she had not got it. A European gentleman (one of the Red Cross) had given her the mark note the evening before, in payment for her fee of two dollars, and had asked for change. She had got the ten dollars off Hassan and paid the man back eight. Hassan spent the next two days searching for the man, without success: he had gone off to attend the wounded. But this did not deter him. He got hold of a Somali policeman, who arrested the woman and took her off to prison, on condition that he had a share of the proceeds. Rather than languish in prison she was forced to sell everything she possessed to scrape together six dollars. (In the end I gave her the money back, and that was the end of Hassan.)

And then there were the spies. In face of the impenetrable discretion of Abyssinian officialdom it was from your spies that you got most of your news. Servants and interpreters were usually Abyssinians. Spies might be Armenians, Greeks, Arabs, any hanger-on who could pick up a rumour in the bazaars. Some of them earned as much as ten pounds a week for the job and were bribed from the service of one journalist to another. Each morning they came to you and told you stories, always sensational, often fantastic, occasionally traceable to a vague substratum of truth. The Emperor had ordered that all the old men should stand in the forefront of the battle, so that they might be killed off first. Twenty-four Japanese staff officers had landed secretly at Berbera and were proceeding to the Ogaden Front. There had been a mutiny among the Boy Scouts, which was put down single-handed by the eleven year old Duke of Harar, armed with a machine-gun. Five hundred Italian officers had deserted to the Abyssinians. And so forth.

When your spy was hard up he would have Lij Yasu, the Old Pretender, out of prison (where incidentally he had lain in a state of lunacy and paralysis for years), bring him to Addis Ababa disguised as a female peasant with a load of camel-dung, reconcile him with the Emperor, and put him in command of an Army Corps of women.

If you were conscientious you searched for some confirmation of such fantasies, before telegraphing them to London. If you were not you telegraphed them to New York as they were, only more so. In the end the principal spies used to get together, decide what lies to tell the journalists each day, and issue a typewritten news bulletin.

The most engaging (and the most disreputable) of all my spies was Mata Hari. I called him that, not because of his beauty, but because he was a spy to the manner born. He had all the traditional mannerisms: the slinking gait, the covert looks over the shoulder, the secretive and almost inaudible tone of his communications behind a discreetly raised hand. Mata Hari was an Arab. I found him in Harar. He wore a filthy blue blazer, filthy grey flannel trousers, and a filthy orange turban which served also as handkerchief, duster, boot-rag, and general factotum. Mata Hari was the black sheep of a respected family of Arab traders. He was usually in prison. Every penny of the salary I paid him went to bribing or bailing himself out again.

We would arrive at some village in the evening. The next morning Mata Hari would appear with chains on his wrists and the furtive, gleeful smile of a naughty boy on his lips, requesting a week's salary in advance. The money would be paid, he would be free, and he would never complain at the dissipation of his wages in such a manner.

ABYSSINIAN STOP PRESS

On my return to Addis Ababa Mata Hari sent me continuous news bulletins. They were written in a scrawling hand, in a language which speaks for itself. For instance:

THE ETHUPIA NEWS OF THE 11TH SEPTEMBER, 1935. TROUBLES AT 3 P.M.

Soldiers. Fieghts near Bazara doors some of the Soldiers entered Bazara house as some brack heads bloods come out. Bazara Manger great trouble pushed them out.

Dagash Mazh (the local governor) said the Ethupians troops will assault the Italian troops before the time of the rain.

Dagash Mazh regarding to the lecture of the 8th advise the soldiers, regret to say, at 3 p.m. the soldiers to their misfortune and endignity on the peoples, robing the vegetable etc. inequity or equity from the Soldiers to treatment of the nations to robing them, is it equity soldiers.

Truck passed on the leg of one Somalee.

News from the Arabic newspapers, the warfare will be between six Governments shortly.

"The King Hailasally" his Excellency endow the ammunitions for the nations.

Somali Merchant Mahmood Warofaih made trench in his garden and put his money, few day repeat to see his money and not found, at once come mad.

2 *longe White men* Journrar arrived.

After a while Mata Hari got cold feet, as the Abyssinian authorities were down on spies. He suggested communicating with me in code, and this was how he put it:

Pantomime as at prasent time very dangrouse as many Ethupian attectives in the town & outside & *urgently to pantomime* & if you made the pantomime if you wants me to daily write to send you in pantomime for the words.

OLD WARRIOR IN HIS SUNDAY BEST

Abyssinian Children Playing at Soldiers

Eventually Mata Hari's demands for money became so astronomical that I gave him to a colleague. Whereupon I had a long, registered letter in which he threatened to "file a suit case" against me in the British Consular Court.

III

It was soon apparent that it would be difficult, in Addis Ababa, to obtain news which was both reliable and interesting. It was a curious foible of the authorities that they only permitted the correspondents to see Abyssinia at its worst. Addis Ababa is a bastard, semi-European, semi-civilized town, hardly typical of the country. Yet for month after month you were confined there, without permission to move further, except to Harar. Not until two months after the war started were journalists permitted to go as far north as Dessye, still three hundred miles from the Front; and there they had even less freedom of movement than in Addis.

Probably this was inevitable. The Emperor did not want to risk a wholesale (or even a piecemeal) massacre of correspondents: it would not have looked well at Geneva. Addis, where mercenary reward covered a multitude of colour-prejudice, was accustomed to Europeans. But there was no knowing what might happen in outlying parts of the country where the Emperor's writ was uncertain, and where one European was as much an enemy as another.

When the Wild Men from the West began to arrive on their way to the Front the Emperor took the precaution of encamping them well outside the City. He made speeches enjoining on them to kill no white men they encountered on their way to the Front. But when they marched through on the way to their raw-meat orgies at the palace you could gauge from their demeanour their reaction if you ran up against them behind the lines. Mockingly, if they saw you in the street, they made play of slitting the throat with the sword.

You saw certain signs of zenophobia, too, among the Abyssinian officials. Sometimes, as in the unabashed rudeness of the Governor of Diredawa, it was open. More often it was politely concealed. But in a race so suspicious as the Abyssinians it was always latent. Not, perhaps, unnaturally, in view of the type of European adventurer who had tried to exploit their country.

But on the surface all was courtesy. Every assistance would be given you. There was a Press Bureau which you visited, as a sort of conventional rite, each morning. You waited for an hour or so in a bare room with a large map of Switzerland and a few Italian shipping posters on the walls. One day a wit marked Addis Ababa and Harar on the Swiss map, and you saw newcomers studying it with earnest, puzzled expressions, wondering why they had never noticed all those lakes before. You waited for the Press Director to arrive. Menials politely and laboriously noted down your questions, and requested you to return to-morrow, when the Press Director would be there. You returned to-morrow. The Press Director was not there. Your questions remained unanswered. And so it went on.

The Emperor's foreign advisers, until, one by one, they succumbed to the climate and went home, were more helpful. There was General Virgin (facetiously described as the only virgin in Addis Ababa), a courteous Swede, who was responsible for the organization of the Army and for the planned strategy of the campaign; there was Mr. E. A. Colson, an American, who inspired the Emperor's consummate handling of the diplomatic situation, and never made a single false step. There was M. Jacques Auberson, a Swiss expert on international law, who steered him through the tortuous juridical complexities of the League. Without them Haile Selassie (to say nothing of the correspondents) would have been all at sea.

When the war started the Press Bureau became simply a Propaganda Bureau, whence emanated eternal communiqués about Abyssinian victories and Italian losses, together with the latest protest to the council of the League of Nations. Soon you ceased to frequent it altogether.

Before the war started there was plenty of news of a kind. Addis was busy and alive. Recruits, from the ages of seventy to twelve, with shabby uniforms and antiquated rifles, drilled in the streets, on the tennis court of the hotel, in the Emperor's private drive, on every available open space which was not reduced to a quagmire by the rains. Periodically the Imperial Guard impressed you by the efficiency of their manœuvres. There was always something doing at the station. Refugees were leaving for Djibouti (though not in appreciable numbers: ninety per cent of the European population, including women and children remained). After the war started, and seemed such a tame affair, they began to flock back again: all, that is, who were allowed back.

There was news of defence plans. Rumours of general mobilization which the blood-and-thunder barons were trying to force on the Emperor in the teeth of his Geneva policy. The arrival of some new Army from the interior. Rickett and his concession. The opening of the Emperor's new propagandist prison, so very much more comfortable than any of the hotels. Edicts (aimed, equally, at Geneva) about cruelty to animals. "Incidents" provoked by Italian Consuls. The comedy of the arrival of the British Legation guard, so hush-hush that it was instantly assumed to be an entire regiment of Sikhs with a trainload of munitions. Memoranda to the League of Nations. Parades of Yemen

Arabs, offering their services to the Emperor. Loyal demonstrations when arms were issued to the troops. Regulations about air-raids, which sent thousands of the population fleeing in terror to the hills. The Emperor's first broadcast to Europe. The Empress's ditto. Recruiting of mules. Visits of barons from the interior to receive instructions from the Emperor. A day without rain. Religious ceremonies, tawdry but entertaining. The Maskal ceremony, to celebrate the end of the rains, when it rained in torrents as thousands of warriors in dripping lions' manes made bloodthirsty demonstrations before the Emperor.

But when the war started Addis settled down again to a peaceful, humdrum existence. Aden, where I was sent later, showed far more signs of war fever. Addis, when I returned from the Red Sea in January, had become the most peaceful place in the world. To a cable from my editor, "GREAT INTEREST HERE REPORT ADDIS EXPECT AIR-RAID NEXT WEEK STOP RUSH STORY PRECAUTIONS PANIC STOP", it was only possible to reply that if London was panicky, Addis was not.

Even the outbreak of war, when Adowa was bombarded, meant little to the inhabitants of Addis. The Tigré was to them another country. Few of them had ever been there, since roads are non-existent. Few knew anyone who had. War, moreover, was a commonplace in the life of the Abyssinian. He was listless in the face of danger and had a supreme contempt for the military capacity of the Italians, whom he regarded as clowns. (This, however, was not shared by the Emperor or his Generals, who were filled with an anxiety about the future which they took pains to conceal.)

To the journalist it was like sitting in a coffee-house in London, in the eighteenth century, to report a Jacobite rebellion in the north of Scotland. The front was quite as remote, and the communications (apart from unreliable Government wireless and telegraph lines) almost as primitive. For our news we listened eagerly each night, through a fusillade of atmospherics, to the radio from Rome, and endeavoured to strike a balance between that and the communiqués at the Press Bureau.

Only the antics of Count Vinci and the staff of the Italian Legation broke the monotony. They were to leave, one morning, in a special train. For an hour the Diplomatic Corps tapped impatient feet on the station platform. The Legation staff arrived, and proceeded to pack their luggage, including the Minister's pet cheetah, on to the train. But nothing more happened. After another hour the rumour began to get around that Vinci was refusing to leave. Outside the Italian Legation we found that it was true. Harassed Abyssinian officials, in cars, were driving up to the Legation in a stream. Irreverent rumours suggested that the Minister and his Military Attaché were locked in the basement, finishing the Legation's well-known cellar. This was untrue. *The Times* correspondent had bought up the remains of the cellar.

Actually His Excellency and the Military Attaché sat calmly in the Chancery, courteously refusing the continuous official requests for their departure on the grounds that the last of the Italian Consuls had not yet arrived from Magalo and that the captain could not leave the sinking ship. So the train went off without them. The Secretary of the Legation ran away and locked himself in the station lavatory with a revolver, just as the train was starting. But he was extracted, and put on the next train. Vinci and the Military Attaché were conducted to the house of Ras Desta, where they lived (on the food of the Imperial Hotel) until the last of the Consuls arrived a fortnight later.

Rumour said that Vinci was in disgrace with Mussolini, as he had advised him that the Abyssinians would make peace at any price; that he hoped, by provoking an incident in Addis, to reinstate himself in the Duce's favour. But later, in Djibouti, Vinci vindicated his action to me otherwise, in the light of subsequent events. The Foreign Minister informed him in writing, just before the Legation staff was due to leave, that the Consul was within three days' journey of the railway. In fact he had not yet left Magalo and did not receive his cabled authorisation from the Foreign Office to do so until three days after the Legation staff had left. He left at once on his twelve days' journey to the railway, where Vinci and the Military Attaché joined him. There the greater part of his baggage was confiscated. Vinci contended that this deliberate falsehood of the Foreign Minister indicated an intention to keep the Consul a prisoner, having safely got rid of his Minister.

If Mussolini was continuously misinformed as to the state of the country the Legation in Addis was less to blame than the Consuls whom he had posted (as virtual spies) all over Abyssinia. They had instructions to communicate, not with Count Vinci, but direct with Mussolini himself, in Rome. They had carte blanche in the matter of cable expenditure and the extent of their telegraph bills became a legend. The British Consul in Harar told me that the Italian Consul's telegraph bill amounted to as much in three months as his own in six years. Of such an immense volume of information reaching Rome a large proportion must have been irresponsible, especially as several of the Consuls (or Consular agents) were not members of the Service at all, and that Italian judgment is apt to be hasty at the best of times.

The Italians had anticipated an immediate internal break-up when the war started. They were premature.

There was some discontent among the civilian population in the war area, due to the scarcity of food and consequent looting, and among the armies themselves when they did not get paid. A party of correspondents, in a village near Dessye, were approached by the population with gifts of eggs, vegetables and fruit. Knowing the scarcity of food, they expressed surprise. But the inhabitants explained, "We are glad the Italians have come at last. Now you will be able to protect us from the depredations of the Abyssinian soldiers."

There was a revolution in Gojjam, presumably engineered by Italian agents. But it was successfully put down. Otherwise the chief internal danger was from bandits. When the war started the Emperor let all the bandits out of prison to go and fight. But most of them preferred to ravage the countryside, profiting by the absence of soldiery and police. One day a local governor sent for the local bandit chief and suggested that it was time he took his men to the war.

"All right," said the bandit. "What will you pay us?"

"A soldier's pay is five dollars a month."

"Five dollars a month!" exclaimed the bandit in astonished indignation. "You dare offer me, the scourge and terror of the countryside, a paltry five dollars a month. Why, it will pay me better to return to my old job."

And he did.

After the Vinci excitement had subsided the various Red Cross detachments began to arrive. From the beginning there had been confusion about the Red Cross, since the sign had, from time immemorial in Abyssinia, denoted a house of ill-fame. (The Italians might, indeed, have justified their bombing of Red Cross Units as a crusade of moral reform.) The old signs were quickly expunged. Nevertheless the opening of a resplendent central Red

Cross office in the main street caused a certain misapprehension among the inhabitants, who thought at first that the Government was simply providing more up-to-date headquarters for a time-honoured pastime.

The arrival of the various units did little to clarify the situation. All were automatically dubbed as spies. The Egyptian unit, fitted out with mules for the northern front, where there are no roads, waited about for weeks in Addis Ababa before being sent to the south, where mules were useless and lorries essential. The British unit (which arrived with an army of Kenya natives, dressed like crusaders at a fancy dress party) was fully equipped, with up-to-date lorries, for the south. It was immediately sent to the north. Thus each, as far away as possible from its own territory, was out of espionage's way.

There was so much Italian bombing of Red Cross hospitals that the Abyssinians learnt, in time, not to take refuge there. "The Red Cross," they said, "draws the bombs as the trees draw the rain." And they took refuge in the eucalyptus woods. Though there were several cases of deliberate bombing of Red Crosses (notably that of the Swedes), often, owing to the nature of the country, it was impossible to place hospital encampments far enough away from detachments of troops to be reasonably safe. Raiding aeroplanes usually flew high, and the margin for error in aim was wide. But the chief explanation was probably psychological. Abyssinian villages and encampments are more or less invisible from the air. It is easy, therefore, to imagine the reaction of an exasperated pilot for whom the Red Cross was at least a target.

In the absence of any sign of war in Addis Ababa the principal diversion was the internecine strife between the journalists. Hot competition for news which wasn't there brought out all the most bellicose instincts of the hundred competitors.

FIASCO IN ADDIS ABABA

There were continual fights at the radio station, where people cribbed and stole and destroyed each other's messages without scruple. Once an Armenian spy sneaked into the office with a message, after closing time. The correspondent of a worthy English newspaper caught him and proceeded to kick and belabour him for some twenty minutes, despite comic protestations regarding his "parole d'honneur." After twenty minutes undignified buffeting the Armenian turned to his aggressor and said, "Be careful, now, or you will provocate me." Later he told me that he had planned to satisfy his honour with revenge. He hired some men to beat up the English correspondent while he slept. But he thought better of the idea.

The chief occasions of disagreement were the meetings of the Foreign Press Association, where you discussed, in theory, grievances against the authorities but, in practice, grievances against one another. These meetings provided an unanswerable argument against the feasibility of a League of Nations (at any rate at eight thousand feet). The French were perpetually "insulté" because of American or English breaches of manners towards them, because they had not been placed properly at the Emperor's banquet, because they had not been given medals; at every meeting they resigned in a body and were coaxed back. The Germans complained that no one could speak their language and they couldn't translate the communiqués. The Americans complained that the English treated the proceedings with too great levity. The English complained that the Americans took things too seriously. The committee was continually resigning and re-electing itself. The one word of sense, in all the meetings I attended, came from the Spaniard, who moved a motion "that there be more news." Thereupon, despite his protests, he was at once elected a vice-president of the association. The meeting always ended in pandemonium, from which the secretary contrived to word some unanimous request to the Government for improved facilities. The Government politely acknowledged it, and that was that.

The only situation on which the Foreign Press Association became really unanimous was the great censorship row. Censorship of telegrams was not introduced until several weeks after the war started. The sensational messages which were emanating from Addis Ababa (including one to the effect that the city had been bombed, with five thousand casualties) made it imperative. It at once raised a storm of protest, less against the principle than the manner of its introduction.

A few weeks before there had arrived in Addis a heterogeneous detachment of Belgian officers. They came partly to succeed the recognized detachment which had trained the Imperial Guard, but was obliged, at the instance of its Government, to resign on the outbreak of war. They were a mixed lot, not countenanced by their Government and not much caring. The Emperor gave them a joint contract and various jobs. One of them, who only knew French, was appointed censor.

Without warning he appeared, one morning, at the radio station and began censoring telegrams with arbitrary gusto, chiefly because he did not understand what they meant. He admitted that he "unspoke English", though from the telegraphese phraseology of his attempts to do so, it was clear that he was trying to learn it from our cables, as he went along. A concerted protest was made. An ultimatum was delivered to the Government that the foreign correspondents would ask for their recall if the Belgian was not relieved of his responsibilities within twenty-four hours. A strike was organized by which it was agreed to send no telegrams pending the Government's reply. But this petered out because too many blacklegs sneaked into the radio station to do so on the sly. No reply was received from the Government and slowly the correspondents discovered that an occasional whisky and soda to the censor met the case as well as any protest. So he remained, and the excitement died. Ultimately he was replaced by another Belgian, who did know a few words of English, and the censorship became reasonable enough.

When I returned to Addis after a two months' journey in the Red Sea and Somaliland, war among correspondents was still the chief excitement. An American correspondent had given a Latvian cinematographer a sock in the jaw, when nerves were frayed on the day of the bombardment at Dessye. The Latvian was suing him in the American Consular Court for ten thousand dollars damages. The case was still going on when I left.

IV

To leave the oppressive, bastard atmosphere of Addis for Harar was always a blessed relief, like leaving school for home.

When I first went to Harar it seemed to me that I had entered a new country. And so, indeed, I had. For Harar is as different in character and history from the rest of Abyssinia as Arabia itself. The difference, as my car passed through the customs gate in the mountains, was as abrupt as a change of scene on a stage. The country rolled away towards the south, rich in pasture, green, fertile, and cultivated with plots of grain, fruit and vegetables.

The road wound past lakes like Scottish lochs, but with flamingos reflected in their waters. Further on the mountain sides were terraced as in Italy or the South of France, but for coffee instead of vines. For the Harar coffee, especially when blended with that of Mocha, across the

Red Sea, is the best in the world, and is exported in large (but not nearly large enough) quantities to Europe and America.

I breathed the air of a land of milk and honey. The hard, barren Amharic country which I had left behind seemed to fall from my senses like an oppressive weight. Not only the scenery, but the actors were different. Harar is the country of the Harari and the Galla people, an amiable race of peasants, easy-going and friendly by comparison with the suspicious, hostile Amharas who have conquered them. Their weapon is the plough, not the sword. They are domestic, not bellicose. They ask only to be allowed to cultivate in peace the garden of Africa which is theirs. They have cultivated it as the Italians will cultivate the Amharic uplands.

The town of Harar itself suddenly appeared beneath us, large, but completely walled, a neat and harmonious entity, as though placed intact on the hillside by a single hand. Here, for the first time in Abyssinia, was a town, not a mere conglomeration of native hovels and European shacks. Here were streets: a bewildering network of them, high and narrow, but well-built and on a coherent plan. The houses were of mud, but they were architecture, not mere huts.

There was colour in the streets. The monotony of the Abyssinian dirty-white was broken by the deep reds and greens and purples of Moslem costume. Arabs and Somalis gave the place a cosmopolitan air. To me, fresh from the wilds of Addis Ababa, Harar seemed more than a town. It seemed a city.

It was a city, indeed, as far back as the seventh century, when it was founded by Arab immigrants from the Yemen, in Arabia. It became the capital of a Moslem city state in the sixteenth century. Such it was when Sir Richard Burton, disguised as an Arab, visited it at the risk of his life three hundred years later. Later Egypt, made great by Mohammed Ali through the early years of the nineteenth century, occupied Harar for ten years. Then, for two years, the Union Jack flew there. The British nominated and supported the Emir Abdulla as ruler when the Egyptians evacuated the city, and it was assumed that it would ultimately come under a British mandate like the rest of British Somaliland.

But all this was changed by Ras Makonnen, the father of Haile Selassie. Acting under Menelik's orders, he drove out the Emir and conquered Harar, where he remained as governor until his death. Thus Harar, once a proud and independent Moslem state, fell under the oppressive domination of a black Christian Empire.

Here Haile Selassie was brought up, together with Lij Yasu, his rival for the throne, whom he was ultimately to overthrow: the one a sensitive and highly-strung youth, devoted to his books and to the European culture which he imbibed at the French Mission, the other a rough young bully who lost no opportunity of discomfiting his cousin at riding or shooting and even, on several occasions, tried to put him conveniently out of the way. Père Jerome, the bearded French Patriarch who educated Haile Selassie, is still there. He is eighty-four, and for fifty-three years has lived in Harar. With touching faith he assured me that this was not going to be a cruel war. The Italian Consul had assured him that aeroplanes and gas would not be used. He believed him implicitly.

Gradually the Amharic colonial infiltration into Harar proceeded, never popular, but resignedly accepted by a people who had no love for fighting, and preferred an easy and civilised life in their ancient city and their richly fertile lands.

In time Haile Selassie himself succeeded his father as Governor of Harar, and won the love not only of the Amharic chiefs and officials but even, to some extent, of the Harari Moslem population to whom he was an alien.

But the loyalty of the Somalis, who extend from Harar to the Ogaden, has always been questionable. The Emperor wisely relied only on Amharic troops, to defend this province. The Somali hates the Abyssinian and in Jijiga I talked to a big Somali chief who said that he wished, with all his tribe, to migrate into British Somaliland rather than fight for the Abyssinians. If the British would not admit them they would go over to the Italians and fight for them.

The Somalis alleged that the Italians, in the Ogaden, had taken a number of Somali women and shipped them to Eritrea, for the entertainment of the troops. If this is true it was a foolish error. The Somalis are inclined to be friendly to the Italians. But to a Moslem women are sacred, and such an act would be unforgivable.

Amharic colonisation has never been popular here, and there is little doubt that, now the Italians have succeeded in dispersing the army of Ras Nasibu and driving the Amharas from Harar, they will find it easy to pacify the province. It seemed, at the time, a strategic error to concentrate their campaign in the North, where the country is barren, instead of making their main drive for these rich lands, so admirably suited to European settlers.

V

The exodus of correspondents began about the beginning of December. For five months newspapers had been spending hundreds of pounds a week on special correspondents with instructions to report a war. Not one of the special correspondents had seen a shot fired in battle; only a few had seen a bomb dropped. The newspapers began to realise that the game was not worth the candle. One by one we were recalled. One by one we sold our unused medicine chests, our mule caravans and our camping outfits. One by one we paid off our servants and our spies and our interpreters, paid our last calls on the Legations, sent our last messages from the radio station, caught, for the last time, that train to Djibouti. One by one, until a mere half dozen remained.

I was not sorry to go. I could only carry away a superficial view of Abyssinia. The war has been successful, partly through the use of gas, but mainly because of the Abyssinian soldier's lack of any real stamina, and the demoralization which spread from one baronial army to another. Now it is over, the Abyssinian will certainly be better off than before. I saw a fraction of a country whose mineral and agricultural resources are undoubtedly rich, but not enough of it to judge how rich. I came to know a little of an ancient "civilization" with a miserably low standard of living and security, in as primitive a state of feudal barbarism as England in 1066. I saw a people to whom a so-called Christian religion has failed to give culture and tradition, and whose Islamic neighbours of Arabia and Somaliland appear, by their side, to be highly civilized races. I learnt (not, perhaps, for the first time), that the "noble savage" is a myth, and that primitive races are obsessed by all the craftiness, avarice, cruelty and suspicion which for some reason we are apt to attribute only to the more advanced and complex stages of civilized man.

But if my impressions of Abyssinia were unsympathetic they were redeemed to some extent by my impressions of the Emperor. Calm, dignified, cultivated, Haile Selassie was a lone beacon of enlightenment in a dark country. He attempted consistently to lighten the darkness. He tried to build roads, to reform justice and prisons, to spread education. He began to abolish slavery, but had not the money, the authority or the organization to do so on any scale.

His more emotional critics were apt to forget that you cannot abolish slavery without providing alternative support and employment for the slaves. Further slavery reforms had, in fact, been drafted, but were delayed by the war. It was not adjudged a suitable moment to let loose thousands of freed slaves on the countryside.

There is a further aspect: that it is hard to abolish slavery until the slaves have been taught to want freedom. The majority, if they serve good masters, are far more contented and secure in slavery than the freeman who has to pay for the greater part of his goods in tribute to an extortionate overlord. Dr. Zervos, the Greek Minister in Abyssinia, was once, to his great embarrassment, presented with two female slaves by a chief who entertained him. He could not refuse the gift, so freed the slaves. Some years later, on revisiting the chief, he was surprised to find the ladies back in their owner's household. "What were we to do," they explained, "without our kind papa to provide for us?"

Haile Selassie realised that his country could never be civilized—could never, indeed, become a country—without European help. Struggling against odds to develop it, he was obstructed in his design on every side: on the one hand by the corrupt priesthood and the blood-and-thunder big chiefs of the old school, in resolute opposition to all progress; on the other by his new and European-educated generation, defiantly nationalist, seeing in the prospect of European influence the doom of its own personal ambitions, of its hunger for an administrative power which, by its own deficiencies of character, it could not wield.

Italy tried, for many years, to penetrate Abyssinia pacifically. She did not adopt the most tactful methods. She failed, resorted to war, and her war succeeded.

It is probable that this people, for whom only force has meaning, could never be civilized without it.

ABYSSINIAN "FORT"

ITALIAN BOMBERS OVER AMBA-ALADJI

THE CRAZY WAR

By MORTIMER DURAND
War-Correspondent to the "Daily Telegraph,"
with the Italian Army in Makale.

F

THE CRAZY WAR

I

BEFORE I could get my typewriter to the Abyssinian bush, I had to wait nearly a month in Italy for permission to go to Eritrea, and during this wait did a few stories on various parades, the mobilisation, etc.

Misfortune befell me when I went to Naples to watch troops embarking. I explained myself at the police office, and was led into the dockyard by an official, who took my credentials to the chief. When he emerged and handed me back my papers, he said I was free to stay and watch as long as I liked. My plea for some written permit was waved aside as quite unnecessary. Had not the chief given permission? Photographs? But, of course. We parted with smiles, hand-shakes and polite bows, and I wandered off to get my story.

The embarkation was much like any other, but the behaviour of the relatives and friends, who had come to see their soldier lads off, interested me. The women who were being left behind for the most part stood dumbly, slow tears welling in their eyes and trickling down their faces; and there were wet eyes among the men on the jetty, too.

It may be my damned insularity, but some of the farewells smacked of the operatic stage to me. I watched two officers clasp hands and stand for a while gazing into each other's eyes in what should, I think, be called a speaking silence. Then they kissed each other fervently on both cheeks, held one another at arm's length for a long, last look, gazing with the air of strong men fighting down their natural emotion, and then one of them turned with a half-suppressed gesture of renunciation and marched steadfastly up the gangway.

At sunset the H.Q. staff arrived, and as I was manœuvring to get a photograph, I felt a tap on the shoulder. Looking round, I saw a diminutive Neapolitan plain-clothes policeman. He wanted to know.

My credentials meant nothing to him, and I was led off through a barrage of hostile and suspicious glances. I felt no qualms, since my credentials had already passed muster, but my confidence was dashed when the portly and pasty-faced chief, to whom I was led, pointed out that according to my passport, I had left Italy a few weeks previously without having ever entered the country.

Unfortunately, I was carrying a notebook containing jottings of prices, instructions from the office and so forth, and the detective had seen me note down a name or two. The task of explaining cryptic notes taxed my powers of hierology (and invention) so much that I felt the prison walls closing round me. Hours passed while I tried to translate the untranslatable into a language with which I had only recently acquired the merest nodding acquaintance, until the chief yielded to my importuning and led me to the police headquarters to wait while he telephoned the Ministero in Rome.

After a considerable time, he re-appeared in the room I was shut in, and with a click of the heels, a fascist salute, and a most courteous flourish, handed me my papers and passport, saying he had made enquiries and established my genuineness. He apologised for the trouble I had been caused, but pointed out the fault lay with the frontier officer, who had stamped my passport "Uscita" instead of "Entrata." Then he waved a hand and a short, swarthy figure emerged from behind him. This was the interpreter, who proceeded to interpret with a strong American accent.

"Chief says you can beat it, but you gotter behave yourself! See?"

He obviously thought I was getting fresh when I said I was in the habit of behaving myself, but that what concerned me now was how I was to get the stupid mistake on my passport remedied. He reluctantly translated to the Chief that I was asking about my passport; and the Chief, now convinced that communication with me was far better than it had been when I was using my halting Italian, indulged in a rapid flood of Neapolitan, the words Uscita and Entrata recurring frequently in the spate of his eloquence. After some minutes, he stopped, and waited while the interpreter translated.

"Chief says you better watch out. You can beat it, now, but you be careful!"

He looked quite taken aback when I told him I didn't believe the Chief had said anything of the kind.

"Ask the Chief," I told him, "what I am to do to get this mistake put straight. That's all I want to know. All this trouble may happen again somewhere else."

The interpreter glared at me, and turned surlily to his Chief. This time, he more or less translated. There came another flood of eloquence, and when it was spent, the swarthy little man said, "Chief says you're right. You better ask in Rome. You can beat it, now, but you gotter watch your step."

II

The accommodation for the foreign correspondents in Asmara was a number of corrugated iron huts in the grounds of the Hamasien hotel. Each hut had four rooms and a water-closet containing a basin and a cold shower. There

85

were two journalists to each room, whose furniture consisted of two beds.

For a time, there were three beds in the room I slept in, which had to house myself, a Spanish journalist, and another Briton; but the latter eventually struck and moved into a different hut. Later, the Spaniard left, and Herbert Matthews of the *New York Times* moved in to share the room with me.

The most unpleasant thing about our accommodation was the lack of proper sanitation—one became conscious of this at a range of ten yards or so from the hut. Another difficulty was the water supply, which was inclined to be temperamental; and I soon learned it was the height of folly to soap all over at once under the shower. The smell encouraged one to get washing over as quickly as possible, but after finding myself for the second time well lathered from top to toe under an unresponsive rose, the water having stopped running for the day, I realised the necessity of steeling my nose while I washed more slowly, piecemeal. On more than one occasion, I shaved and washed with a bottle or two of mineral water brought from the hotel.

The huts were electrically lit, but a secondary lighting system of candles stuck in bottles was essential, since Asmara's electrical supply was as fickle as its water.

The Press office—"Ufficio Stampa"—was the Fascisti headquarters, a big hall, whose walls were decorated with Ethiopian mural paintings (one panel obviously Jonah being spewed up by the whale) very primitive in execution, and if they had any artistic merit, it would need finer perceptions than mine to discern it.

Asmara is a town which could be quite a little beauty spot. Its weather in the dry season is as near perfection as anything you can imagine, hot without being oppressive in the daytime, and wonderfully cool at night. A coat is desirable soon after sunset. But the place naturally suffered from a huge influx of people for the campaign, it was not designed for such a large population.

Palms, tree-cacti, bougainvillæa and some yellow flowering shrubs do their best to make the town decorative, in spite of its red brick Cathedral and the dust. By night, the streets are not illuminated. There is nothing to do there.

From the first day, I felt ill from the effect of the altitude and although I was told this strange, unpleasant sensation of dizziness and lassitude would wear off in a fortnight, it never did, nor did a constant sensation of breathlessness.

One effect of the altitude was that I always slept badly. On the first morning a kindly German correspondent looked in through the window of my room and asked how I had slept. When I said not very well, he inquired,

"Ach, there was in your bed a little animal?"

I was able to assure him to the contrary; no such company graced me till the occupation of Makale.

At first there were no restrictions on our movements except transport difficulties. It was a day or two before I could get passage in a lorry, but it was at length arranged, and I set off about dawn. I carried a map bought in London, and for a time tried to use it; but I had not gone on many trips before I gave it up as hopeless. There is as yet no such thing as an accurate map even of the Tigré, unless the Italians have already completed their surveys, which I think they can hardly have done up to the time of writing, and there is most certainly no accurate map of Ethiopia. The dust alone made the journey abominable, without counting the complaining of bones and muscles after ten hours or so at a fast speed over newly constructed, military roads, which made it necessary over and over again to hold on tightly to avoid being thrown out altogether.

Kit and supplies were not infrequently hurled out at particularly bad places.

Soon after leaving Asmara the dust began to make things unbearable, settling softly over my hands and face, powdering my clothes, getting into my eyes so that the lids of them seemed to grit on my eyeballs, filling and choking mouth and nose, and setting up a continual irritation at the back of my throat.

Later in my stay out there, I found the bronchial irritation almost insufferable at night, when the temperature had tumbled from several degrees over a hundred Fahrenheit to a degree or two above freezing point. Then, whether I was in my small bivouac tent, lying on a waterproof groundsheet on the ground, or rolled-up under a bush, the dew on my blankets glistening back at the crisp stars, a little, maddening cough would come and would not be denied. I have known it hold off the sleep of exhaustion for hours.

The dust had an acrid taste that seemed different from and worse than any other I have eaten. It was a finer variety than any other I had met. "Polvere" the Italian word fits it perfectly. It lay several inches deep on the roads, rolled softly away from the wheels of lorries like the bow waves of a ship, billowed up beside them, and rose in their wake in a smoke-like plume, to hang in the still air for minutes before gradually dissipating. On the roads all faces were grey masks, grim and ghost-like.

In some parts of the country, the dust was red instead of grey but it tasted just as nasty. Vegetation by the roadsides was being choked and killed for fifty yards or so on each side. In a fairly fertile plain which I crossed later on a journey to Adua, I saw a great sycamore lifting bare branches from its gnarled trunk, only a handful of withered leaves left drooping.

THE CRAZY WAR

If you brush your hand against a stone by the road-side, the dust on it will cling to your skin as though it were damp—an effect of its fineness. Whenever I got out of the lorry and walked through dust, I found that when I wanted to climb in again, I had to kick my boots to shake off caked clots of the fine powder, which had the consistency of Fullers' earth. Of the many parties of road-workers we passed, labouring with picks and shovels on the stiffest problem the Italians had to solve—communications—quite a number were simply pouring shovelful after shovelful of dust over the precipice side of the road.

These men, whelmed in clouds of fog-like dust every time a lorry-train passed them in the streams of transport, were sometimes stripped to the waist, in which case there was a continual conflict between dust and sweat on their torsos, many wore goggles against the dust but found, I was told, great trouble in keeping the eyepieces transparent, while a number worked with a rag tied over nose and mouth. I adopted the last measure myself, tying a handkerchief round my neck loosely, so that whenever we passed another lorry I could pull it up to keep the dust out of my nostrils, to some extent at least.

My discomfort on this journey was forgotten in amazement at the landscape. I seemed to be travelling through a nightmarish land that only a god of hate or a mad god could have fashioned. The high plateau is seamed with vast crevices, so that Abyssinia seems a country that stops short suddenly after several miles of travel, to go on again hundreds of feet higher or lower. I remember my surprise at one point when I thought we were going along a plain slightly less barren than most, but suddenly saw that a hundred yards on our right was a sheer drop of about a thousand feet to another plain, out of which an amba of bare rock, hundreds of feet high, stuck up like a colossal tooth. On a later journey, an American colleague remarked that the scenery "beats the Colorado canyon."

The light is strange in Ethiopia, and it tricked the professional photographers at first. I had noticed there was something queer about it, because the landscape seemed so colourless except at a few minutes about sunset. Even in the glare of midday, the stops to use were what you would have on your camera for a sunny English summer's day.

Many Italians, I found, were very much puzzled that Italy should be spending so much for such a place. At one place where we stopped for a while, there was a party of road-workers on their job, and one of them after glancing at an amba that stuck up like a sore thumb out of a barren plain, lifted the grimy rag over his mouth and nose, and said, "Perché . . .Why do we want this country?" Neither I nor his work-mates could tell him.

Other Italians are eaten up with their own heroism— a common malady, if one can use such a term for a quality of that kind, which often causes them to do astonishingly brave but frequently misguided actions.

On my first trip, I had a talk with an Italian soldier, which contrasted sharply with the young road-worker's pessimism. My lorry was held up for a long time at a particularly difficult place, where the rough road snaked up the mountainside in a series of tight hairpin bends, by a long lorry train which stuck for an hour or more. All up the twisting way were immobile lorries with rocks behind their wheels, and the only thing that moved was a small red "dust devil," whose tall column danced up the road.

The soldier strolled over and asked me for a cigarette,

and when he had lit it asked where I was going. "Entiscio," I told him, "and you?"

"No," he said, "Addis."

"After you," I remarked. He drew himself up, and spoke imposingly.

"I am a soldier. I come here to die."

When I told him I had come there to watch him do it, a lot of explanation was involved; but we parted friends, saying we would meet in Addis.

Close to the top of this mountain we passed an Ethiopian hamlet of the flat roofed kind of huts. The walls were of big stones cemented with earth and cow-dung, and they were built squarely against the side of the mountain so that the back wall, though rather a sloping one, was ready made. The roofs were roughly thatched and covered with mud. From the doors and from the roof tops, women were watching the stream of lorries. They were dressed in dirty white shamahs, and their fat-greased hair was neatly ribbed fore-and-aft, the thin crisp ribs of it closely following the contour of their heads from brow to the nape of the neck, where it was frizzed out in a puff. One of the women outside the huts was carrying a long-handled parasol, whose small, flat umbrella was made of wicker-work. A black boy passed close beside the road, followed by a dog that had rather the look of a beagle, and he gave us the fascist salute.

As far as I could make out from my map—and as I have said that was pretty hopeless—this hamlet was called Addibacle, and the mountain, Amba Toquile. From the top of it I looked over an immense panorama, and my first impression was of a vast desolation. The distance was full of mountain-peaks and mountains cul-minating in flat tops, and the sides of the nearer ones were spotted with scrub; then foot-hills dropped to a great plain, more thickly scrub-covered, from the midst of which reared a huge, forbidding amba. The only trees in sight were the giant cacti, Euphorbia Candelabrum, lifting their curved gaunt, spiny arms thirty feet into the air. Not even the changing beauty of cloud-shadows that dappled this immensity could soften its grimness.

By evening we reached our goal, General Pirzio Biroli's headquarters, in the Edaga Sunni valley, Entiscio. I was longing for a wash in the stream, Mai Unguia running a few hundred yards below the camp, but the fact that some Italian soldiers were well under way watering mules there put me off. Looking back from half way up the hillside, I saw that I need not have been so fussy, as a few yards down-stream from the watering places, a number of Italians were washing themselves and their clothes, while still a little farther down-stream, Askaris were filling dozens of water-bottles for drinking purposes.

General Pirzio Biroli is, as an American colleague of mine remarked some months later, "the hell of a swell egg," a burly, magnificent horseman, and the type of sportsman who lays himself out to put a foreigner at his ease and to give him all the help he needs. Of course, there was to be no nonsense about the rations in the lorry: dinner would be served in the mess tent shortly, and meantime what about a wash? An Askari brought a big water container and poured water for me to wash, others were sent down to the lorry for the kit.

Seeing my eye had been caught by an Askari doing some primitive cooking at a camp fire, the General sent for him and his "Borguta." This was the Askari's bread, which he was baking by rolling dough round a stone and putting it into the glowing base of the fire. I tried a bit, and found it solid eating but not unpalatable, though its fire-blackened appearance was against it.

The informality of the mess surprised me at dinner, which was much better than what I had been having in Asmara, and I in turn surprised an Italian captain by not liking to light a cigarette afterwards because the general had not yet done so. Later, I was to see the general standing and chatting with a group of officers, two of them very junior ones, who remained sitting perfectly at their ease.

I had not yet become accustomed to Italian discipline, and I must admit that I never quite did.

III

General Alessandro Pirzio Biroli, wearing a light cloak of grey over his shoulders against the chill of dawn, appeared at the tent of his headquarters mess. He had turned out to see me off on mule-back for the front line.

"How did you sleep in the Ritz?" he asked me as cups of black coffee were brought from the kitchen, a structure of poles nearby, covered and partly walled with leafy branches. I assured him I had slept excellently on the ground of the tent in my "flea-bag."

Tiny Abyssinian mules, no bigger than donkeys, were waiting for two officers and myself with a guard of four Askaris, cloaked, with their tall red tarbouches khaki-covered. Only the red and blue tassels hanging from the tarbouches and a glimpse of their sashes gave colour to their uniforms.

There was no barbed wire nor any other protection round the camp, for the Abyssinians will not attack unless led by their chiefs. The chiefs, as I had seen at dusk the night before, were not inclined for fight.

In an open square tent Colonel Della Porta had sat at a table receiving the submission of the natives. An old man with a grey beard, a forked stick in his hand, walked out of a crowd of about one hundred white-robed Abyssinian men, women and children, some of whom had curled up to sleep under the bushes on the hillside. From the folds of the robes on the backs of the women a small, inquisitive black baby's face sometimes protruded.

The old chief bowed to the colonel, who inquired his name, so that a clerk might note it on his typewriter at a table near by. Then the chief, an important personage in the district, waved his hand to a youth behind him, and the youth stepped forward leading a white-and-brown goat, which bleated protestingly.

Placing his hand to his heart, the youth bowed; and the colonel, accepting the gift-goat, exclaimed, "O, molto bello!"

Such scenes as this one, I was told, were customary every day, and not the slightest fear of an attack on the camp was entertained. The natives were not then deprived of their arms, but the chiefs are held responsible for their good behaviour. Every man, woman and child made submission personally—they preferred to be on the safe side.

The sun was still hidden by a mountain-top on the other side of the Edega Sunni valley, and I shivered as I mounted my mule. We passed the wireless masts of headquarters and pushed on up the hillside till we met the sunlight, when suddenly we were warm. The sun struck hotly when we reached the top of the plateau.

On the way up I noticed markings on rock-faces, which reminded me of the "cup and ring" marks, dating from prehistoric times, to be seen in Argyllshire and elsewhere. The marking consisted of six dots in three regular lines, cut in flat rock-surfaces.

"That is an Abyssinian game" the Alpini major who

was guiding our party told me, "but it is only played by bambini, not by grown men."

We came to cultivated ground, and in a field of crops I saw a small black boy sitting on a platform made of sticks and grass, supported on four poles some eight feet tall. He was shouting a series of wild calls, and I learned that he was a scarecrow and sentry combined.

When we reached a newly begun road we had to draw aside to allow a mule-train led by Askaris with red and green sashes and tassels of the 20th Battalion, to pass. They were followed by a few camels laden with tents, picks and shovels. The mules were carrying farina, a meal for bread-making, in sacks, and boxes of tea, coffee and sugar.

While my guide and the officer in charge of the mule train were talking, the Askari guard behind my mule slipped into a field near by and began gathering something. He returned grinning, said, "Molto bene," and shelled some little peas into my hands. They were delicious, but when the major caught sight of them he was not pleased. The Abyssinian farmer, he pointed out, would be very angry if he knew.

I noticed the passing Askaris had rifles of different sizes. "Some are still armed with Mannlichers taken from the Austrians in the war," I was told. "Those are long and heavy, and fire only five shots. Most nowadays have had these replaced by the regular Italian rifles, which fire six shots."

We resumed our march along the track of the new road, passing narrow terraces of cultivation on the mountain-side. On coming through a mountain-pass, we saw a valley with huge rock outcrops in it, but well cultivated, wherever possible, and apparently quite fertile in spots.

Across the valley, over the hills on the opposite side,

appeared the fantastic mountains of the Semien range which always seem to haunt the horizon in these parts. They are almost caricatures of mountains, great towers and pinnacles of upthrusting naked rock, which have no business outside a futurist scene-setting.

I looked into one of the native huts we passed. Its round walls were built of big irregular stones, the cracks being filled with earth and cow-dung. A baulk of timber was placed on top across the middle, and a king-post on this supported the point of the conical thatched roof.

There was no chimney, but a flat stone served as fire-place in the middle of the floor, which was of mud on wooden baulks. A raised platform a few inches higher than the floor had straw on it for a bed. The rest of the furniture was a number of big earthenware pots.

Rough stone blocks as steps led to the door, which was made of two wide baulks of timber, one being cut to form an upper and lower hinge turning in apertures in the stone wall. Two or three huts usually huddle together, surrounded by a low stone wall surmounted by a rough fence of sticks to prevent hyenas getting in at night and stealing babies.

Under the floor of the hut was a stable for cattle or goats, to which access was obtained by a door at the side, so that this primitive building was two-storied—ground floor and basement. There was nobody at home but a very small black boy. The grown-ups were at work in the fields. As the bambino took a marked dislike to me and the Askari soldier with me, we left hastily.

A number of large Sicilian mules, chained two and two, passed us when we resumed our march. These, I learned, were sick mules going back for rest. The casualty list among mules is a high one, for mules are the hardest worked creatures in Abyssinia. The sure-footed,

FIELD WIRELESS—ABYSSINIAN STYLE

FIRST POISON GAS—THEN DENTAL TREATMENT

BEEF FOR THE FRONT LINE

tiny mule of Abyssinia can manage country which defeats the European kind.

The headquarters of the 2nd Askari Division, for which we were bound, was now in sight on a spur of Amba Aughier at a great distance, but only a few white tents were visible. Most Italian tents are cleverly camouflaged a russet brown and green, which fades into the background.

Coming to a plain, we encountered a body of Askaris on manoeuvres, with machine-guns and cavalry. I noticed their colours were carried with them. On some rocks a group of natives in their dirty white robes squatted watching.

"Whenever we have manoeuvres," the major told me, "the natives always watch very closely. Afterwards they talk it over for days and days."

In the plain were good fields and grass and big trees, but vegetation grew sparser as our gallant little mules attacked the rocky track on the other side. A line of barefooted Askaris with fixed bayonets overtook us, under the command of a smart Alpini officer with brown gloves and a monocle. He wore the coloured sash of his battalion of Askaris round his waist.

An extraordinary noise broke out from the head of the small column, which at first I could not identify. Then, at one of the continual twists in the track, I saw that the three leading Askaris were playing long flutes. Subsequent examination showed that one of these was made of metal, the others of wood bound with leather, they are called Mbelti.

To my ears the music just missed form, though often I thought I caught a hint of melody. The flute players went straight up the precipitous track, playing unconcernedly as though sitting at ease.

Said the Alpini officer: "We always have music on the march. That tune is the regimental march."

I thought it wise not to return the hint of a smile in his eyes when he used the word "tune." Later I was glad, for I heard an Askari whistling that tune and realised that its form was fogged by the wails and groans of strange harmonies when the flutes played them.

So we arrived at headquarters close by the Wrara Pass with something of a flourish.

IV

At General Pesenti's headquarters, close to the Wrara Pass, I saw the arms captured from the defending Abyssinians when the pass was taken a few days before. There were venerable brass-bound horse pistols, one with a crown and the word "Tower" on it, one French made, and old rifles, mostly sporting patterns, which would have taken a braver man than me to fire.

The colonel who had led the advance up the valley told me the defenders fired one scattered volley and threw down their arms. There was not time for many casualties.

Now the "prisoners of war" roamed about the Italian camp chatting with the Askaris and quite free to come and go as they liked.

The front line was a series of low stone walls, apertured for machine-guns, near which bare-foot Askaris with red and yellow tassels hanging from their tall tarbouches, squatted holding rifles across their knees.

One of them had lit a small fire and was brewing tea in a blue enamel pot. Tea is the favourite Askari drink and a pot like this one often finishes off their equipment on the march. They also usually carry canes with crooked handles, the use of which I was told, is to clear the ground in front of their bare feet of snakes. I never saw one do this, but then I never saw a snake out there at all.

Half a mile in front of the pass, at the bottom of the Wrara valley below, a hamlet of conical thatched tuculs, surrounded by rough stone walls, sprawled about a clump of tall eucalyptus trees among cultivated fields and hay stacks.

An outpost had been flung beyond the trees, and during the day time the Askaris' supply mules were led down between the front line and the outpost to graze.

The Italians had captured a three years' store of Ras Seyum's ammunition in the last advance, and a report had just come from one of their Ethiopian spies in front that he had located another dump. A second spy was at once sent off to join him, with orders to stay there till the next advance.

The reports of Ethiopian spies, were occasionally accurate, but they usually told fantastic tales calculated to please their new masters. While I was talking to the Italian officers one spy came in to report that he had seen a letter from the Emperor to Ras Seyum chiding him in the strongest terms for not having defended the Tigré. Ras Seyum was supposed to be in the Tembien district, the mountain peaks of which peeped over a high plateau on the right of the valley.

A hundred yards behind the pass, under the lee of the Amba, sat the staff colonel, under a gaily striped awning, in front of which was a mast flying the regimental colours.

He was receiving the submission of fifty natives who had come in to surrender, bringing gifts of goats, eggs and chickens. He told me that this was a daily routine and while we talked a gift cock strutted round our feet and punctuated the conversation with crowing.

A few yards away an Askari barber was shaving the mutton-fatted black scalp of a soldier. It looked a painful proceeding, and I asked an officer what he was using for the operation.

"An old razor-blade that one of us has thrown away," he said.

Many Askaris are very vain of their appearance. As I passed through the camp on my way to the front line I noticed one of them, lying in a little bivouac tent, regarding himself in a small mirror and carefully greasing and curling his long moustachios. I was about an hour up at the pass but when I came back again he was still at it.

The short descriptive I tapped out that evening went over field radio to Asmara, and as a precaution a copy went by courier as well. It was lucky I took that precaution. The radio message received by those liaison press officers, Count Bosdari and Marchese Gonzago who were always extraordinarily helpful to me, puzzled even their bright brains.

"Novo averlookring iwarna" it began, described the position as, "lin louful sceune" and spoke of "grey robed wives some borbies esaks fronte cotolets."

The last bit of this referred to a very tragic sight. On the previous day, there had been sniping behind the lines. Two Askaris watering their mules, were shot dead. The Italians had rounded up eleven Ethiopians and were waiting for permission from headquarters to shoot them. I saw their wives and families file up to the colonel's awning led by a Coptic priest. Many of the women had little babies slung on their backs. Some money was given to them so that they might live while their husbands or fathers were awaiting sentence.

v

The second time I saw Amba Aughier was from the air. When I eventually got back to Asmara, I learned that there was a possibility of a few journalists being allowed

to go on an air reconnaissance and I at once proceeded
to make a nuisance of myself. I told Count Ciano, the
Duce's son-in-law, and the late Baron Ostini, who was a
man of great personal charm, that I had been a pilot,
and begged and bothered until I got permission to go
down to the aerodrome and at least see them take off.
Before dawn next morning I was on the landing ground
where the three machines were already lined up. They
were Caproni bombers of the "La Disperata"—Death or
Glory—squadron, which Count Ciano leads.

At the last moment they said I could come along and
I climbed gladly in.

The formation blared and bumped its way across the
landing ground, took off and headed for Entiscio. There
was no gunner in the after machine-gun position under the
tail so I made myself comfortable in this position, where
I could get a very good view of the terrain below and
was out of the wind.

We passed over the Wrara Pass, which was then the
spearhead of the Italian advance and having crossed
the range at somewhere near ten thousand feet the machines
dipped a little and flew at about 110 m.p.h. towards
Makale which was then, of course, still in the hands of
the Ethiopians. There was a patch work of cultivation
in the valley, and the little clusters of tuculs—in hamlets
which surround the town—looked like patches of little
brown bubbles on the dust brown surface of the earth.

On reaching the town the formation broke up and the
machines circled low over the roofs. Most of these were
flat thatch and mud covers to square whitish stone huts,
some were conical thatches, only a few had corrugated
iron roofs. The white, octagonal, Coptic church had a
corrugated iron roof, and there were one or two on two
storied houses near Ras Seyum's ghebi. This was a brown,

four-towered castle, whose surrounding wall had tumbled down in several places.

From my position in the tail I could clearly see the Abyssinians squatting at their machine-guns, while others were quickly rushing guns into position. As we circled, the Abyssinian gunners opened bursts of fire. The second pilot of my machine flung himself on the machine-gun and replied. Occasionally I caught glimpses of the other machines as they swooped and fired on the guns below.

After a short action the aircraft resumed formation and went on with its reconnoitring over Amba Adai.

The village of Adi Aidaro seemed desolate, as the inhabitants had apparently taken to their houses, perhaps thinking that the thatched roofs could offer them some protection.

We then turned and flew back over Makale, where the Abyssinians again opened fire. Count Ciano's adjutant, Captain Casero, afterwards told me he calculated that fifty machine-guns had been firing at us.

Over Makale our formation again dispersed and we circled low over the town returning the Abyssinian fire. I saw one machine-gun crew break up and run for cover, their gun having presumably been put out of action.

Resuming formation after this second action we flew in the direction of the Tembien district, where Ras Seyum was supposed to be waiting with a large army. Passing north of Adi Abbi, we flew over the deep canyon of the Tecazze River towards Cela Ceccanu.

Here the formation again broke up and the machines flew low over the twisting, precipitous gorges and razor backed mountains thinly peppered with scrub. The brown rugged landscape seemed appallingly desolate, dreadful as the mountains of the moon.

I saw only a few fields in pockets of the barren country

where were tiny patch works of green and brown cultivation, and very occasionally the bottom of a mountain slope was ribbed in terraces of meagre crops.

There was not the least sign of any Abyssinian forces. If Ras Seyum's army was there, it was cleverly hidden.

Our return flight was over Axum, with its eucalyptus trees and the famous tall monolith, over the miserable hovels of Adua, and across the Mareb River back to the base. In this flight the formation had covered four hundred miles. Not one of the machines had so much as a bullet hole in the wing to show for the engagements.

VI

When the news came through that the advance on Makale had started there was a wild rush and clamouring for transport by all the correspondents and photographers in Asmara. Matthews was away with the Danakil column, but I was lucky enough to get a place in a lorry which my friends the American photographers, Joe Caneva and Rousseau, "swell eggs" with whom I did many trips, Warhurst, The Times photographer and an Italian photographer had got hold of. We were badly held up by lorry trains and later by mule and camel trains but reached Negasc on the evening of the second day. General Montagna, in command of the "October 28th" Blackshirt division entertained photographers and journalists that night at a dinner table made for the occasion by bearded blackshirts from a pile of rocks.

Dawn saw us on the move again, doing a great deal of marching beside our lorry as roads were practically non-existent.

We stopped for lunch on a flat plateau covered with yellow grass, and an old Abyssinian priest in a dirty white

103

robe and black fez came up to talk to us. I offered him
a piece of cheese but he spat it out in disgust. When
Rousseau gave him a handful of boiled sweets, however,
he bowed deeply, in gratitude. He was also very pleased
with a piece of tinfoil, which he carefully wrapped round
the handle of his goat-hair fly-whisk; and as we went
on we saw him collecting all the tins we had thrown away.

Our approach to Agula was down a very steep torrent
track in which the lorry stuck. While the others cast
right and left over the rock-strewn hills covered with
camel-thorn to try to find another track, the Italian photographer and I laboured sweatily with rocks, and after a
couple of hours had widened the stream bed enough and
had made a good enough road to get the lorry down.

We passed a hamlet of tuculs just above Agula where
the Abyssinian maidens greeted us with their high trilling
call, mistaking our lorry, the first that had passed that
way, for part of the advancing cohorts.

I pitched my tent that night near the headquarters'
tents of the Askari battalion which had just arrived at
Agula. Next day I left my companions and walked across
the ford to where Ras Gugsa's irregulars were camped
at the foot of the mountain by the tracks leading to the
Selat Pass.

Seeing a crowd of Ethiopians round the front of a tent
I went up to find out what was going on. A tall, young-
looking Italian officer was jabbering away in Tigrine
with them and beside him was a clerk with a type-writer.
The officer was Dr. Franco, the consul who had been
imprisoned in Adua, and he was now assessing the price
of damages claimed by Ethiopians who had joined Ras
Gugsa, and whose huts had in consequence been destroyed
by Ras Seyum's men. Dr. Franco sat on the ground at
his tent door, and the blacks in their grey robes, with

their long rifles, sometimes brass-bound, and their scimitars squatted in a small dense crowd before him. He broke up the conference to talk to me, and after a few minutes I heard a great hubbub.

"Abiet! Abiet! Abiet!" chorused many voices in unison.

"Because I sent them away to talk to you," laughed Dr. Franco, "they are discontented. Now they have assembled in front of the Ras's tent and are demanding an audience."

"They are not a bad people really," he told me, "though they are very dirty and nearly half of them are diseased. They have a sense of justice; and their methods of calling your attention are picturesque. Sometimes when I go out of my tent, I find a native lying on the ground face downwards in front of it, with a big stone resting on the back of his head. Naturally one asks what he is doing. Then he explains that just as that stone was oppressing him, so is some injustice weighing upon him and he has come to me to right his wrongs."

Suddenly we heard an outbreak of confused shouting and saw the natives rushing about in a wildly excited way. We went outside and saw an aeroplane coming over the mountains behind Agula. It fired coloured parachute lights as signals. And then we saw the Italian hosts winding along the scrub dotted hillside, dark lines of men with only an occasional glint of the sun on rifles showing that they were armed.

Groups of tanks roared and crashed down the gully, where I had laboured to make a road for my lorry, and lined up on the plain of Agula.

I hurried back across the Agula stream, where men were working feverishly to make a ford of rocks, to find out if the advance was to continue that evening. To my embarrassment a small band of about a dozen Ethiopian Irregulars, with rifles and scimitars, attached themselves to me and firmly ignored all my efforts to send them away. They had evidently decided that I was an Italian officer and a heaven-sent leader to follow to victory. Several Italian officers looked dubiously at my "command," and I did my best to look as though they were not of my party; but when they followed me right into the headquarters' camp I was forced to appeal to a mumtasc (corporal) of Askaris, who dismissed my retinue with a stream of well-chosen Tigrine.

The Agula valley, in which a few hours before only the calls of the Askaris were to be heard, soon began to hum with the low roar of voices of the newly arrived troops.

.   .   .   .   .

Next night I wrote my despatch by the light of a camp fire on the central heights overlooking Makale. To right and left the other two great Amba ends of the plateau above the valley towered like fortresses. The camp fires of the advance Askari companies sparkled under the bright moon. The main bodies of the Italian troops were far in the rear.

Before dawn at Sellat, I looked across the Agula valley and saw the plumes of smoke arising from camp fires, as though the surrounding hills were on fire.

The Askari companies each with a Shumbashi bearing a pennant were the first to cross the ford. I deserted the Irregulars, to whom I had attached myself and marched with the Askaris. Getting across to the long column winding up the steep mountain track put me farther behind the advance guard than I cared to be, so I had to make pace in order to pass gradually up towards the head of the column.

It was a stiff climb towards the pass and the sun topped the hill as I got there. To the west I could see the line of white-robed Irregulars threading their way upwards.

The pass was held by a guard of Irregulars squatting with their long rifles between their knees. They got up as the pennants approached and raised their rifles in salute. The long khaki line was fringed with the coloured tassels of the Askaris' fezes and pricked by the pennants. Each company was led by officers on mule back.

At 8.30 we reached rolling broken downland with yellow grass, sparse shrubs and occasional stony fields of tall millet. Yellow thistles and "Queen Anne's lace" decorated the parched ground, and among the rocks were little wild flowers of many colours.

We advanced towards a sloping hill topped by a thirty foot rampart of purple rock arising straight across our paths like a barrier.

I was travelling as light as I could, I had left my tent behind at Agula and was carrying only my overcoat rolled up in my blankets with a tinned food supply and water bottle, but even this was more than I wanted to carry. Gradually I became aware that a quiet voice behind me was steadily saying, "Monsieur . . . Mister . . . Herr . . . " over and over again. I turned round to see one of the Italian officers on a mule smiling down at me. He asked if I would not like to put my load on a pack mule, and as by then I was close to the head of the column I was glad to accept his offer, which was followed up by a drink of coffee from his vacuum flask. Later on another officer offered me a stick of chocolate, and yet another, cognac from his flask.

Irregular camp followers walked beside the troops. There were women with reddened finger nails carrying black ewers, a boy with an elaborate silver-plated dish on his head and others with long-spouted coffee pots. A wooden chair, of office type, with a hole burnt in its seat was borne on one youth's back. Another boy caused roars of laughter among the Italian officers, because he was carrying like a helmet on his head a utensil common enough in bedrooms but incongruous and unexpected on the march in Ethiopia.

We toiled up the steep rocky paths and descended into a valley where there were good wheat crops. Then came more broken country with cliffs dropping away to the left.

At eleven we halted for watering. The Askaris (and I) robbed an onion field. The soldiers also uprooted some dead branches which had formed a fence and carried them on their shoulders for lighting that night's camp fires. I hate onions, but I lunched off seven, taken with sardines and sweet biscuits, that day.

Passing groups of Irregulars squatting with their long rifles and scimitars beside their mules with gaudy silver trappings and blue and scarlet saddle cloths, we climbed to the top of a mountain. Below, a tremendous view of rolling hills stretching to the distant mountains, burst upon my gaze.

In the fields, Abyssinians were crouching, cutting their corn with sickles, quite unperturbed by the Italian advance.

The steepest of all our climbs was up the final rocky track through thick shrubs and clumps of flowers which looked like Michaelmas daisies. When we reached the summit the Italians at once began to erect wireless masts.

I now learned that this division was not going to enter Makale next day but was proceeding eastwards to Dolo; and at this juncture I ran across a colleague, John Whitaker, of the *New York Herald Tribune*. We joined forces, and fearing that some other troops might be going into Makale that night, we humped our packs and struck westwards, trudging right across the Italian front, in no-man's land, as it were. We moved carefully, keeping out of sight as far as possible, as we were afraid the Italians might order us back. All went well, though we were both feeling pretty tired, until we reached the right flank. There a mumtasc and a file of Askaris arrested us, but we luckily learned that their captain was reconnoitring to westwards. So we assured them that the Colonello had sent us to the Capitano, and they were eventually convinced and let us go. During the hour or so before dark we made sure that no troops were advancing into the Makale plain. There was no sign of any of Ras Seyum's forces. So we made our weary way back to the central Amba end, and there a colonel in command of Askari troops invited us to supper. I was already in my blankets under a bush and nearly asleep when the invitation arrived but it was impossible to refuse. We supped by moonlight off ammunition boxes.

VII

In that strange campaign in Ethiopia, over a terrain of crag and precipice, where Nature seems to have lost her temper with the landscape or to have become demented, things happened which in any other war would seem fabulous.

The invaders occupy a large province almost without firing a shot and they march peacefully, without even taking the normal precautions of piquetting heights and so on, through places that are natural fortresses, where one would think a handful of men could hold up a battalion. When they are consolidating positions and developing communications, fighting begins behind their lines.

Anti-aircraft guns fire downwards at bombing aeroplanes—as happened when Count Ciano led "La Disperata" squadron to attack an Ethiopian camp in the Buia valley.

Oerlikon guns opened on the aeroplanes from the mountain-sides above. There seems to have been no tactical reason for the squadron to dive so low—it was just a piece of typical Italian heroism, which often seemed to me to militate against the taking of simple precautions.

One of the strangest phenomena of the campaign was the escape of Colonel Mariotti's flanking column from a perfect ambushment in Enda Gorge, near Azbi, where Degiacc Cassa Sebat's force held it for a day.

The purpose of the column, which my friend Matthews accompanied, was to protect the left flank of the main Italian advance on Makale.

The band of Thio, 100 Danakils under Second Lt. Pirami, joined up just as Mariotti was leaving. They had made a forced march of three and a half days across the salt plains, but there was no time for a rest. Mariotti's force set out, 2,000 strong, all Askaris or Danakils—about half of them boys of sixteen or eighteen—under tried Colonial officers, some of whom had had sixteen years' experience in Libyan campaigns.

The column was carrying four chests containing 10,000 thalers, and 10,000 rifles, to be presented to a force of Danakils which was expected to join up before they reached the well at Elefan. Thirty camels carrying four mountain guns followed, and the supply train. The column was always in fighting order, as an attack was expected.

It soon became apparent that the maps were very inaccurate; unmarked mountains were encountered and sometimes where mountainous country was indicated there would be a plain.

Mariotti gave out false information for the benefit of Sebat's spies, announcing, for instance, that he would camp at Lellingheddi, whereas he passed on to Au. At night the guns were mounted, heights about the camp were occupied and sentries posted.

No Danakils joined before the column reached Elefan, but shortly afterwards they appeared. Instead of 10,000, however, there were only 200 of them. All the time, confusing reports of Sebat's movements and intentions were coming in.

The white officers were stared at in amazement by the groups of inhabitants passed on the way. At Elefan, where natives were interrogated, only one old man had seen a white man before—and he was doubtful, because it was the Greek shopkeeper in Makale he had seen, and the old black was not sure he counted as white.

No answer had been received to a letter written from Damallé by Mariotti to Sebat, telling him to submit or take the consequences, and at Au it had been learned from chiefs who made submission, that he was preparing to attack with a force that was not composed of natives of the district. Where and when the blow would fall, no one could foretell. Sebat was said to have 400 trained men and 100 Irregulars.

Mariotti's column left Au at dawn on the 12th. He was already behind time, since Makale had been occupied three days before. After nearly four hours' march the column reached a small gorge, half a mile long and very narrow, running East and West.

The dry bed of the Enda river ran along the bottom, the sides were precipitous, Mount Lugbu formed the north side, Mount Derdega the south. Fifty yards up the side of Lugbu a mule track ran. The other end of the gorge was practically closed by a slope of the northern mountain.

During the three hours' climb towards this gorge the progress of the column was accompanied by an insistent, reiterated, clear bird-call of two notes on the left flank. Afterwards officers thought this must have been a signal.

The column entered this gorge, instead of halting and bringing up the guns, without even taking the precaution of piquetting the heights. The flanking files, composed of men from the band of Massawa, were only thirty yards up the mountain-sides on either flank of the main column.

The vanguard, composed of the rest of the band of Massawa, followed by the band of Thio and the 200 Danakils, commanded by Colonel Belly, had almost reached the eastern end of the gorge, and only the supply caravan, protected by the rearguard of the 26th Battalion of Askaris, were still outside it, when Mariotti suddenly exclaimed that the place was a perfect one for an ambush. He called two orderlies, sent one forward to halt the van and the other back to summon the captain of the camel battery.

When this officer came up, Mariotti gave him the order to bring up the guns and train them on the ridge in front.

As the captain saluted there came a crash of musketry from three sides which echoed round the gorge so confusingly that it was impossible to locate the enemy concentrations. The artillery captain fell with a bullet in the ankle.

Twenty-three out of the thirty camels carrying the artillery were shot down, and in the first volley the crew of one gun were killed. The Italian sergeant served and fired a gun all day, single-handed.

Colonel Belly, who was sixty-two years old, was wounded in knee and hand by machine-gun bullets, but led the van to the attack in an uphill charge. Hand-to-hand fighting ensued, but the column could not force the end of the pass. On the north flank the Ethiopians reached the road

News-Reel Camera more Interesting than War

RED CROSS TENT AT DESSIE BLOWN UP BY ITALIAN BOMB

before being driven back—largely by the use of hand grenades.

Five machine-guns were playing on the Italian column, in addition to Mauser rifles and rifles presented by the Italians in 1928. It transpired that the end of the gorge was only lightly held and that the main Ethiopian forces were on the flanks.

For a few terrible minutes it seemed as though the black soldiers of the Italian forces would break and run, and only the example and exhortations of the white officers and Askari non-commissioned officers rallied them. The young Askaris became wildly excited and rushed about, their tall tarbouches being brushed off in the shoulder-high scrub until the ground was littered with them.

The Askari non-commissioned officers produced lions' claws, and strips of lion-skin and exhibited them, boasting of the lions and men they had killed and exhorting the men to be lions in battle.

At the beginning Italian officers were saying, "Let them shoot! They have only four or five rounds each, and then we'll attack." But they soon realised their enemies were well supplied.

Firing continued spasmodically all day long. Twice a reconnoitring aeroplane flew over without sighting the column in its desperate straits. The band of Massawa was only able to hold its own, and the 26th Askari Battalion, attempting an attack from the rear of the position towards the flank, could only get part way up the mountain side. They had placed the few remaining camels and the supply-train mules in a position by a cliff out of fire.

At intervals all day an Ethiopian trumpeter blared defiance with mocking trumpet blasts, a sound which afterwards Italian officers said was the worst thing in the whole action. After some hours every blast drew a volley and even bursts of machine-gun fire, as the men's nerves frayed; but the trumpeter was well hidden in a cave and he was never hit.

Mariotti prepared for a last stand and retreat. For three and a half hours the action hung in the balance, but no further attacks came, only the rifle fire of an invisible enemy and the derisive sound of the trumpet.

And all the while, Degiacc Cassa Sebat and his staff could be seen through field-glasses on a distant amba top, well out of range, calmly watching the progress of the fight.

Night fell and firing ceased. Mariotti ordered no fires, no smoking. The portable radio set was put into commission. Signals for help were broadcast, Adigrat, Adowa, Asmara were called—but there was no reply.

Then Colonel Mariotti, speaking the very language of that heroism to which I have already referred, said: "Nobody hears us. We are abandoned by all. Let us hope that God has not abandoned us!"

No shot was fired all night, and just before dawn Mariotti said: "We cannot stay here. We must gain the heights. Another night here means destruction."

All were convinced the Ethiopians were waiting for them, but as a last desperate attempt the Colonel sent the van in single file up the hillside. Heavy losses seemed certain, but the alternative to this was destruction.

Carrying wounded, picking up wounded who had lain exposed all night, the column moved slowly on.

Not a shot was fired. The Ethiopian force had vanished in the night. And though the column left its supply train far behind and was without food four days, the only other casualties suffered were among the wounded they carried with them.

The High Command sent aeroplanes to drop food by

parachute for the column. Looking back on Azbi, when more than half a day's march past the town, the column saw the aircraft busily dropping supplies. Doubtless the natives enjoyed them.

VIII

When the history of Italy's invasion of Ethiopia comes to be written, I wonder if any mention will be made of two khaki-clad white men, who were waiting at the foot of Amba Enda Micael for the advance on Makale, and who led the left line of Ras Gugsa's irregulars for several miles across the plain.

Perhaps in future "Fantasias," when the blacks with song and dance recount their prowess, those two mysterious figures will assume supernatural proportions. Their exit will perhaps be in a cloud of fire over Makale.

Whitaker and I were roused from our heavy slumbers under our bush on the heights overlooking the Makale plain by the chanting of a shumbashi (sergeant) waking his askaris in the darkness before dawn, and I had the pleasure of hearing the Italian colonel, shortly afterwards, ticking off one of his officers in generous terms. In a high voice, shaking with passion, he almost screamed: "This is the second time this has happened. If it happens a third time, I shall kill you with my bare hands, and face court martial in any court in the world."

We followed the bobbing lanterns of the Askaris through the darkness, down the steep track to the plain, the morning star in our faces, and then struck right to intercept the advance on the town.

The sun came up over the mountain range behind us, and the air began to lose some of its chill. As we topped a low spur at the centre of the three cliff-like ends of the mountain, we saw in front of us the rough stone walls and conical thatches of the hamlet called Ariena. Some Ethiopians with long rifles slung on their shoulders were moving about among the huts, but we saw a black girl come out of a tucul carrying on her head a bulbous water-pot with the neck stuffed with straw, and this "business as usual" atmosphere reassured us.

Our arrival created a stir, and I began to be afraid our reception might be hostile. A young black lad ran to fetch the chief, however, and we sat down on some rocks to wait and see what would happen next. While we were waiting I hired a small black boy to carry my roll of blankets. It had to be a very small boy, because as soon as an Ethiopian is big enough to carry a rifle or scimitar, he will not demean himself by carrying burdens—that is for women, old men or children. I once induced one to take my pack and let me carry his rifle, by giving him money, but after about a hundred yards the youngster suddenly sat down on the track and refused to look at me or to speak. His shame had overwhelmed him, and further offers of cash did not avail to restore his amour propre.

From where we were sitting, Whitaker and I had a fine view of the plain of Makale. Cultivated fields stretched across to the mountain, behind the western spur of which the town was situated, and almost straight across our path ran the stream which goes on to Dolo—the Mai (river) Dolo. Directly south was a walled house built of brown stone, with a low square gate-tower at its eastern end, which had a few eucalyptus trees grouped about it. On the spur of the mountain hiding Makale, the dun-coloured *tuculs* of a village called Sciafat were clearly visible. There was no sign of any Ethiopian forces—Ras Seyum had evidently wisely decided on discretion for this occasion.

The chief of the village appeared with two or three more warriors, all with slung rifles, and we did our best to talk with them by signs. When they understood we wanted to go on to Makale, there was an outburst of chattering. The chief pulled aside his *shamah* of dirty grey and pointed to the red and yellow cartridge belt round his waist. There were eight empty places in it.

"Makale!" he grinned meaningly. Then, raising his hands as though he had a rifle, he said, "Hou! Hou! Hou!" And he shook his head at us, and rolled his eyes warningly.

Another warrior quickly thrust himself forward, held up his left hand and counted on his fingers up to thirteen. "Makale!" he said triumphantly, striking his chest with his fist, meaning he had killed five more men than his chief, who did not look pleased.

I stood up then and repeated, "Makale," nodding. A great jabbering ensued, the chief laying a detaining hand on my arm and shaking his head violently. At this difficult moment a youth came up with a wicker bowl in his hands. The chief took it from him and with a courtly gesture presented it to me. His dignity sat well on him —he was quite a fine looking, rather Arab-like type. I did my best to keep my horror out of my face when I saw the bowl was full—there must have been a good pint and a half of goat's milk in it—and that there were a good number of drowned insects floating on the surface; but with a quick aside to my American colleague to the effect that he was in this too, I did my part, insects and all. Whitaker groaned when I handed the bowl on to him.

I then offered the chief a cigarette, which he took with an air of pleased interest. He blew out the first match I held up for him, so I signed that it was necessary to

suck in. When he did so, the result was unfortunate—
he made a face of acute disgust, coughed, threw the cigarette on to the ground and spat. But a few seconds later,
he picked the cigarette up again, pinched it out with his
fingers, and tucked it away inside his shamah.

We tried to get out of our difficulty by signing that
we were not going to Makale, but to another village we
could see to westwards—its name was Lacci—but the
chief and two warriors insisted on escorting us. We
went down a precipitous track, and found when we reached
Lacci that there was a big gathering of warriors and elders,
all very puzzled about us, but prepared to be friendly. We
sat on a low stone wall while they crowded round, and
did our best to talk by signs. Another bowl of milk was
brought, but I could only manage a mouthful. I made
friends with one youngster by admiring his rifle—it was
Belgian-made, and had the Ethiopian lion and some
Amharic characters engraved on it. Our friendship was
sealed when I presented him with two wax matches,
which he evidently considered valuable treasures, and I
was glad to see how pleased he was, because for some
minutes a black had been sitting beside me on the wall,
sharpening an offensive looking, crooked knife on the stone
and another had been sitting beside my colleague, doing
the same thing with a bayonet.

I managed to explain that Gugsa was coming to Makale,
which caused a great buzz of excitement, in which I heard
the words "Hailé Selassié Gugsa" repeated, and my state-
ment was fortunately underlined by two reconnaissance
aircraft flying over. This resulted in what appeared to
be a meeting of Parliament, and we took the opportunity
to move on.

It was now about two hours after sunrise, and we made
the best pace we could over the broken ground towards

the western cliff-face of the Amba. As we approached it ten Caproni bombers roared over, and almost immediately after we saw the white robes of the leading irregulars of Ras Gugsa's forces coming over the top of the mountain.

We made haste to intercept them, but they reached the bottom before we could get across. They halted there for us, however, and, when we came up with them, greeted us with hand-clapping—naturally thinking we were Italian officers.

Their leader was a picturesque, bearded fellow, dressed in breeches and a chocolate-coloured pullover, and wearing a scimitar. He made signs asking us to lead his line, and so we set out side by side at the head of the column, with a scout about five yards in front of us.

After about a quarter of an hour we saw that there were two other lines of irregulars on our right, moving parallel with us across the plain. From each little cluster of huts on the Amba sides all round came the high, far-carrying call of welcome, a trilling sound made by the women.

My colleague dropped back down the line to try to find out if it was going to enter the town itself, and so I, an Englishman, was left for some time "in charge." Actually I merely followed the scout, though once when I saw that we were drawing ahead of the other two lines, and that the rear of my line was straggling, I turned and held up my hand to halt the column for a few minutes. When the alignment was correct I led my irregulars on again.

After crossing Mai Dolo we approached fields of tall millet, and I was relieved to find that some dark objects I saw among the crops were only rocks.

Then a Fitaurari, a minor chieftain, rode over to us from the centre line—he was extremely puzzled by me—

and directed the left line towards Sciafat. The padding of black feet quickened to a jog-trot, and the line swung eastwards. As my goal was the town, I abandoned my "command" and joined the centre line to be the first Briton to enter Makale.

.   .   .   .   .

Near the big four-towered castle of Makale is what corresponds to the village green—an expanse of baked earth. In the middle of this is a subsidence ten feet deep with precipitous sides, presumably the village pond, but in the dry season of course bone dry and used by the inhabitants as a casual rubbish dump, though rubbish is seldom really dumped, it is left where it happens to fall.

A miniature canyon, eight feet deep in the parched earth, represents the village stream along one side of the green, and on the other side of this is the shop, a stone building of two stories with a corrugated iron roof.

The shop enjoyed a day's boom when Makale was entered by the Italians. Approaching it in the evening, I found a small crowd of soldiers trying to get someone to open the strong high double door. With the help of two Italian officers I managed to get in and a few of the soldiers slipped in quickly. The door was then hurriedly slammed and secured by a baulk of timber wedged against a huge rock on the stone floor inside.

There was at first a marked reluctance on the part of a young man of complicated descent to serve anybody with anything. He was inclined to deny that there was anything to sell. Finally the proprietor was produced, a very ancient Greek, dressed in dirty khaki, a cloak and forage cap. His bare legs under his shorts were covered with weals and sores. Gaining his confidence was a lengthy business. His shop had been twice raided, he told me subsequently, by Ethiopian troops, and he was not sure that the Italians might not treat him badly too.

I wanted food, but food was definitely "off." He could not imagine how it would be possible to obtain a mule. With the greatest reluctance he admitted that a bottle of vermouth and a bottle of brandy on a dirty shelf might be bought for thirty lira each. I noticed the brandy bottle had the label of a highly superior English firm and also that the seal had been tampered with, but my Italian friend decided to risk it.

I wanted a small aluminium cup I saw on the shelf, worth possibly twopence. When he understood I was willing to pay for it, the Greek's methods of salesmanship came into play. The cup was not for sale and he did not want to part with it. In the end he let me have it as a favour for twenty times its value . . . but only because he was very fond of the English.

The Italian officers and I went into a garden behind the shop to eat a hurried snack of biscuits. When one of my friends tasted the brandy, he spat hastily and threw the bottle on to the ground. A strange smell, reminiscent of petrol, methylated spirit and aniseed arose.

Here I again met Dr. Franco, and invited him to share our repast in the garden of the Greek's establishment. The young diplomat was concerned as usual with matters of justice.

"There is another shop behind this garden," he told me, "where they are selling sugar and other things to the soldiers. The prices they are charging are enough to make your hair stand on end! This will have to be looked into."

It was looked into. At dawn next morning I came to make another effort to get a mule and something to eat. Two carabinieri were on guard at the big doors. The

Greek's brief day was over and Makale no longer had a shop.

And that is the reason why I had to start off in the morning to get back to Asmara with nothing but a wine bottle filled with dirty Makale water and my blankets. My few remaining tins of food, and my water bottle had all been stolen as I slept.

After wild but ineffectual efforts to buy a mule at any price I was faced with the necessity of starting back to Asmara on foot, and so I set out across the Makale plain.

On the way I made several efforts to buy a mule from Ethiopian farmers, as I suppose they were, but beyond giggling in a silly way because they could not understand the strange tongue of the white man, and signing that they would guide me to some mythical "Agula" to westward of my route they gave me no help. I went on then, up the pass and made the best pace I could for a few miles along the track leading to Mai Mecdem. The silence was eerie. Apparently no supplies or reinforcing troops were using this route.

For hours I did not see even a wandering Ethiopian. I remember at one point being delighted at the sight of some birds, one of which flashed through the sunlight like a flying ruby, another long-tailed variety reminded me strongly of an English magpie, but its voice was croaking and harsh.

My only food that day consisted of some ears of corn which I plucked as I passed through a stony, infertile field. I half filled the aluminium mug I had bought from the Greek with these grains, poured the perilous Makale water on to them and after letting the mixture soak for a while got it down my throat.

Abruptly, my left foot gave way under me, and I sprawled down full length. Some years previously, I had damaged this foot doing a parachute jump and it was never quite the equal of my right foot. The third day's forced march was too much for it.

I had to lie up among the rocks and think of the stories my rivals would be getting off when they got in touch with communications.

I remember looking up at a euphorbia, lifting its silly prickly arms into the silent air, and saying aloud, "Why the hell don't you grow telephones on you, you flickering chandelier?"

After a while I tried my foot out and found it held, and so I began to hobble back towards Makale, utterly heartsick at my failure.

I met nobody until I had climbed down the pass again and had limped half way across the plain. The sun had set by then and the air was growing cold. I met a party of three Italian soldiers, who immediately fell upon me, and even while they questioned me as to what the dickens I was doing, grabbed the blankets off my back and one of them put his arm round me, making me put my arm round his neck, and so helped me back to the nearest officers' mess.

Here a subaltern gave me some soup and the corner of a shed to lie down in on a heap of straw. I wrote my despatch by the light of a hurricane lamp and sent off two copies by couriers, who happened to be going Asmara way.

Next morning, I succeeded in buying a tiny Abyssinian mule with a wooden Abyssinian saddle at a starvation price, and hugging my glass bottle which I had refilled with dirty Makale water, started off again across the plain.

Half-way across I was overtaken by a posse of French and Italian journalists with an escort of blackshirts. They were horrified at the idea of anybody traversing the country without adequate military protection, and as the black-

shirt officer was obviously going to cause trouble I had
to fall in with them and go to Dolo, where wheeled transport
back to Asmara was awaiting them.

When I eventually dragged my lame foot up the steps
of the Ufficio Stampa, I heard something which nearly
broke my heart. The first of my despatches had never
arrived at all, the second, sent three days previously,
had anticipated my arrival by only half an hour.

It was dysentery for me after this.

IX

How far Solomon, the black boy who was supposed to
clean out my hut in Asmara, was really responsible for the
rape of the turtle I shall never know now, but I am willing
to believe anything of him. He always remained slightly
mysterious in his crookedness, because there was no
common ground between him and his "Padroni." I am
sure he was no thief in the ordinary sense, for, as he once
protested to a British correspondent, he often found money
lying about in his room and always returned it.

Solomon had religion taped. He professed himself a
Christian, and so attended all the festas of the Church,
but happily accompanied his Moslem friends when there
was anything good doing in the way of celebrations in their
faith. The only drawback to this arrangement was that
he could not follow the example of one of the Moslem boys,
who, his American master assured me, always got out his
praying mat at the first hint of any work in the offing, and
carried out an almost interminable series of prostrations.

Though not a thief, as I have said, Solomon was an
advanced type of borrower, and sometimes his borrowing
was quite altruistic. On one occasion, shouts of fury
came from the next room to mine with answering yells

from Solomon and a rather elderly British correspondent burst in saying, "Tell him I'll kill him!"

Between Solomon and this Briton there was a great gulf fixed, because the reporter blandly ignored the Tower of Babel. As far as he was concerned, the thing might never have been invented.

It transpired that Solomon had gone into his room, and with a polite "Permesso," had picked up his hair-brush. When stopped, he explained volubly and with appropriate gestures, which got his meaning across, that he only wanted to brush the coat of a Spaniard in a neighbouring room.

Solomon's body was strangely twisted in an angular silhouette from an accident on the Asmara-Massawa road, in which the driver of the vehicle was killed. This fact came to light after an inquiry instituted by some newspaper men, who suspected that he was diseased. He could never obey my repeated orders to talk without shouting, nor could I ever induce him not to burst into the room at any time he chose. Most mornings he would come energetically limping with his dragging shuffle up the steps of the hut, singing some tuneless native song, and burst into the room long before I wanted to wake up. And my sourly grunted, "Go to hell," was invariably met by a beaming smile and, "'giorno, padrone." On those occasions when it was possible to get some coffee from the hotel, I would send him for some, and a few minutes after bringing it, while I was still in bed, he would burst in again, and holding his right arm and twisted fingers stiffly up as though calling God to witness, he would shout, "Caffé latte, cinque lire."

He never could make out our craze for water. Once when I came out of the water-closet-cum-shower, he rubbed his thin chest with a gnarled fist and asked, "Perché sempre lavare, lavare, lavare?"

Suspected of having stolen a number of handkerchiefs, he countered neatly by asking what their owner thought he would do with a handkerchief if he had one.

To go back to the rape of the turtle, which I began this chapter with but got side-tracked, a foreign woman correspondent was found by an Italian reporter standing in front of her hut and surrounded by all the black boys. She was wringing her hands and demanding that the military police should be called out at once.

"You have stolen my turtle," she stormed, "and my turtle and I have been inseparable for four years. Call the Carabinieri, and say they are called for me—for *me!*"

The Italian suggested that before the military police were summoned, a search might be instituted, and asked her where she had last seen her pet. In a casserole, she said, outside her hut, where she had put it to enjoy the warmth of the sun.

Where was the casserole? Here one of the black boys cut in. It was his padrone's casserole, he said, which he had washed and put out in the sun to dry. On going to fetch it in, he found it occupied by a turtle. Accepting this as one of those things that happen to casseroles put in the sun to dry, he shrugged and left the initiative to the turtle. Returning later, he saw the turtle had vacated the casserole, so he took it back to his padrone's room. Not for him to inquire into the comings and goings of turtles.

Madame would have none of this specious tale. It was abundantly clear to her that it was just a part of the plot by which her turtle had been ravished from her, and she had little doubt that one of these black thieves had incarcerated her beloved pet somewhere where he could enjoy the sweets of its company in secret and lonely communion. Call out the Carabinieri!

The Italian prevailed upon her, however, to allow a brief search round the hut and inside it, and when the searchers poured into the lady's room, her darling was discovered under her bed, in a receptacle not designed for the housing of turtles. The re-union, I was told, was very affecting, and all present marvelled at the wonderful ways of turtles.

Somehow, I had a weak spot for Solomon. The black I engaged as personal servant made no such impression on me, he was simply a rather irritating, very lazy nonentity, who never even made me violently angry, as Solomon often did. I cannot remember his name.

While dysentery laid me low, Solomon was much concerned. One evening when I had fallen into a welcome, if rather swimmy sleep, I was suddenly brought to by his croaking yell, and there he stood in the doorway demanding that I should tell him what to do for me. That was easy—go away.

Half an hour later, he woke me again by noisily shutting the window, which I naturally wanted open. After another lapse of time, he came rushing in clamouring that I should tell him to fetch me broth, which he said he could get from the hotel.

He only woke me once more that evening, and that was to tell me he was going to pray to the "grande Dio" for my recovery.

Six weeks or so later, when the doctors sent me down to Massaua, Solomon asked if he could come along and look after me. I was glad to be able to say it would not be allowed.

Solomon was dirty, lazy, a liar and a near-thief. His ways were as tortuous as the dragging shuffle of his lamed legs, his nature as crooked as his broken body. He was one of the ugliest creatures I have ever seen.

But he was somebody's black swan, for he was due to be married about the time I left.

The other fellows sacked him when I was down at Massaua, and they were quite right. Solomon was intolerable. And yet. . . . Oh, well—I'm a reporter and I suppose I saw a story in him.

An Italian Bomber (*above*) and its Abyssinian Counterpart

PRESS LORRY IN DIFFICULTIES

WITH THE LIONS OF JUBA

By EDMUND DEMAITRE

"Excelsior" (Paris), one of the four War-
Correspondents with the Italian Army in the
South.

1

WITH THE LIONS OF JUBA

I.—ON THE SOMALI FRONT.

"Allah is great and may his name be praised!

"I am well and I hope you are well also. I send this letter by my son Abdullah, for I have just heard that you are making war against those sons of dogs who, last year, stole thirteen of my camels. Among these camels was a particularly valuable one which I bought for forty thalers.

"They say in the *sciavelli* that you and your sons command the men who are ready to do battle against the camel thieves, who shall rot everlastingly in Gehenna. Consequently I am writing to tell you that, if you wish, I shall come to you with twenty-seven of my men who are all as brave and strong as the lions of Juba.

"This letter is written by Ali Mohamed who knows the Koran, but it bears also the sign of my hand.

"May the Prophet lengthen your shadow and those of your sons.

"In the year 1313 of the Hegira, in the month of Ramadan.

"HOUSSEIN ABDULLAH."

The Colonel read this letter closely, then turning to the young Somali he said in a grave voice:

"Abdullah, son of Houssein Abdullah, return to your father and tell him that I expect him with his men before the full moon. And may God bless him, and all those who are dear to him. Peace be with you!"

Abdullah bowed deeply and departed with the feline movements of the Somali.

131

"Next," said the Colonel.

Two sentries, wearing the *billao*, the terrifying Somali dagger, led in an old native whose face, black as ebony, was framed in a snow-white beard. Wrapped in striped robes, his hand on the pommel of his dagger, straight as the trunk of a young palm, proud and strong and controlled, this splendid old man made one think of the princes of the Arabian Nights or the Hittite warriors who led the armies of Joshua.

"Welcome to my house, Yussouf!" said the officer.

"You know me?" cried the old man, visibly surprised at such a greeting.

"Who between the Juba and the Webbe-Shibeli does not know Yussouf of Bar-Aber?" replied the Colonel. "Haven't I myself promised a hundred thalers to any one who would bring you here dead or alive?"

"The Koran says," replied Yussouf of Bar-Aber imperturbably, "that when the road is before you it is useless to turn aside from it. Yesterday I was your enemy and you were my enemy. But to-day we can fight together against the common foe. That is why I have come without arms into your camp. If you wish I shall bring you fifty armed men and I shall make you forget the past."

"It is agreed, Yussouf. The past is forgotten. You are appointed *yousbachi* of the *doubats*."

So they come, from the banks of the Juba, from the Marrehan bush, the deserted regions of the Migiourtina, as if a Caliph, resurrected by a miracle, had unfurled the green flag of the Prophet. Young and old, nomadic hunters and peaceful fishermen, worshippers of Allah and savage fetichists, chiefs of the *Kabylas*—or tribes—nobles and ex-slaves, old bandits, and scholars of the Koran, all moving like an interminable flood towards the camps where the *Doubats*, the native attacking forces of the Italian army, are recruited. It is not just a question of avenging insults, pillages and raids. It is not a question of earning five lira a day. It is not a question of atoning for past crimes. What is far and away more important is that war in any form represents for the Somalis the most noble, worthy and significant manifestation of life; the most honourable endeavour, the most poignant and virile of physical and moral emotions.

"Me very happy to fight!" an old Yousbacki said to me one day. And he added, "My father died in war, my father's father died in war. Me have lived like an old woman for fifteen years."

It must be added that psychological factors arising from snobbishness—if one may call it that—exert a strong influence on the mentality of these splendid warriors, inheritors of the valour, the arrogance and the savage enthusiasm of their ancestors, who thousands of years ago, left the arid deserts of Yemen and broke like waves on the burning shores of Migiourtina.

According to the social code of the Somalis there is no greater shame than to earn one's living by physical exertion, and they put the shepherds at the top of their social hierarchy; all their labour consists in lying in the shade of a palm-tree, sleeping or meditating, while the camels and goats crop the burned grass of the bush. In these conditions one understands why, unlike other primitive peoples, Somalis consider the hunters social pariahs, obliged to tramp, run and tire themselves for hours in order to kill a peaceful kudu or a slender-horned oryx. In short, although they know neither the name nor the works of the author of *Man and Super-Man*, the *Weltanschauung* of the Somalis is inspired by Bernard Shaw's pet principles, but modified by other curious influences, for the Somalis, despisers of work, think that, outside the nomadic shepherds, the employeés of the State are the only human beings who do nothing and who are therefore to be considered the true aristocrats.

Italian Somaliland being an exotic country, they insist that the State employeés must know how to read and write. So there is nothing more difficult than for an inhabitant of the bush to reach the top of the social ladder, where are to be found the porters, office-boys, and native customs officials. What can they do to obtain favours comparable to these? They enlist in the army, where knowledge of the alphabet is not required but which gives the same prestige as the Customs, the Post-office or the railways. It is true that in the army one has to work, even work hard. But on the other hand there is the hope of one day being able to cut someone's throat. And when it is a question of cutting throats the laziest Somali belonging to the noblest of tribes is ready at a moment's notice to cover a hundred kilometres on foot! . . .

Here is the explanation of the extraordinary fact that, from the formation of the first battalion of doubats, in a land only conquered and finally pacified a bare ten years ago, one did not come upon a single village, not a huddle of wretched toukouls where the men had not left to offer their arms and their lives voluntarily to the white Mouchir. And the most significant thing of all is that once they handle the rifle or the *billao*, once they are ranked behind the standard-bearer waving the banner of Savoy, they forget all the motives that led them to adopt the white turban of the doubats. They become warriors, and warriors only, wild and daring, deserving the name which they have been given, and which is now famous between the tropic of Cancer and the equator: "The Lions of Juba."

The real lions that lie hidden in the thick bush have no reason to be offended by it. The comparison is justified.

II.—LA CHANSON DE ROLAND OF SOMALILAND.

When night falls and fires are lit in the camps of the doubats, one hears strange tales, fascinating stories of heroes wearing the white turban. . . .

But before recounting these stories, I must emphasise that the burning-eyed men who pitch their camps between Dolo and Gabré-Daré do not consider life on earth as Europeans do.

They attribute no exaggerated importance to the more or less agreeable interlude in eternal existence which we call life, and which for them is only a road leading to Gehenna or Paradise according to whether one is just and good, or "*bilach,*" that is to say bad.

Thus to die is not always *bilach*. . . . It is something which happens to everyone, and is not to be taken as a tragedy. Human life is, in short, a relatively unimportant interlude. This explains the outlook revealed to me by the doubat Ibrahim, come from Yemen to enlist in the free corps.

". . . It is like this," he said to me, "I came back and found him in my tent. 'Do you know who I am?' I asked him. He replied 'Yes.' Then I put before him the praying-mat which I brought from Mecca, and asked him to say his prayers. When he had finished I fired twice, once in his head and once in his stomach. Then I took aim at my wife and put two bullets in her head. It was a pity. . . . She was beautiful and cost me fifty camels . . . but tell me, could I do otherwise?"

"No, decidedly not," I answered after mature reflexion. "But what did the judge, he you call *Cadi*, say?"

"He was as wise as you," replied Ibrahim the doubat politely, "he declared that I could not have done otherwise."

Ibrahim had told me this story in the same tone that he would have used for some amusing little anecdote. Scratching his shaved head, he added, "You know the *Mumtaz* Mohamed? When the war is over and I return home I shall have to kill him. . . ."

"What, Ibrahim, your second wife too? . . ."

"It has nothing to do with my wife," replied Ibrahim with dignity. "Mohamed was my slave. He ran away from Yemen ten years ago and enlisted as a soldier in Somaliland. He has become a *mumtaz*, while I am only a doubat. . . . I said to him therefore, 'You can give me orders and I will carry them out because you are my *mumtaz*. But once we get back to Yemen I will kill you! . . . Tell me, General, could I do otherwise?"

Feeling sure that the *Mumtaz* Mohamed would be flayed rather than return to his country, and being unwilling to contradict my fierce servant, I replied,

"You are right, Ibrahim. You stick to it. But I must tell you that I am not a general. . . ."

"What you say is very *bilach*," declared the servant coldly, "you sleep in the general's tent, eat what he eats, and you have a glass-eye like him. So you must be a general. Sleep well and peace be with you. . . ."

He threw a last furtive glance at my "glass-eye"—that is at my monocle—then, bowing low, he disappeared into the night.

Ibrahim the doubat is no exception. These men kill and die with an exasperating indifference—I would almost say nonchalance—which while it is full of elegance and wisdom, nevertheless makes anyone, who can distinguish between the life of a man and that of a fly, shudder. This explains the mentality of the doubat who, during the battle of Lamascillindi, threw himself in front of Lieut. Stancari, crying,

"You are very good, me die for you. . . ." He received the shots intended for the officer full in the chest and died instantly, with a happy smile on his lips. . . . What shall one say, too, of the man who went quite alone to attack a machine-gun, and overcame all the men in the trench with the exception of one Ethiopian machine-gunner. The survivor managed to turn his gun on the doubat and put half-a-dozen bullets in his chest. Wounded to death, with no more cartridges in his rifle, the doubat flung himself on his adversary and killed him with a terrific thrust of his *billao*. When the other doubats reached the scene of the combat—worthy to figure in the future *Chanson de Roland* of Somaliland—they found their dead comrade clinging to the conquered machine-gun.

"*Ferid*, very good," affirmed the father of the doubat, who was fighting in the same battalion, standing over the body. "Allah is great and he knows what he is doing."

Allah does certainly, but one wonders, and not un-reasonably, if the doubats always realise what they are doing. When the forces of Commander Fava encircled the Ethiopian fortress of Dagnerrei, it was decided that the Italians should attack it from the south, an attack from any other quarter being doomed to certain failure. Three hours before the launching of the offensive, a deputation of doubats came to the commandant.

"The Ethiopians say," declared their spokesman, "that their fortress is impregnable. We want to show that it is not. We want to attack from the north side, the difficult side, to show that the fortress is *bilach*. . . ."

The commandant Fava—a magnificent type of colonial officer—thanked the doubats for their zeal and courage, but, bringing forward tactical and strategical arguments, he declared all the same that they would attack from the south. . . . The doubats were not satisfied. So the officer, knowing that nothing is more dangerous than to shake the faith of the natives in the courage of their white superiors, decided to attempt the impossible. At the head of the doubats, who howled with joy, he set out to assail an almost perpendicular rock crowned with a fortress which was fortified with numerous machine-guns. The assailants were welcomed with a hail of bullets. The doubats fell like flies. It was seven o'clock in the morning. By eleven the Tricolour floated over Dagnerrei.

Would you like to hear the story of the battle of Lamascillindi? Lamascillindi is a small village situated about a hundred kilometres from Dolo on the banks of the Webi-Gestro. It had been occupied several months before by the Ethiopians, under the command of the *grasmatchis* Abba Gouradja and Argaou. The presence of the enemy on the Webi-Gestro becoming strictly undesirable, Colonel Prigiotti determined to occupy and destroy the village, then to fall back on the Juba. Accompanied by Captain Fischetti he set out at the head of five hundred doubats in the direction of Lamascillindi. Twenty-five kilometres from the village the column suddenly had to halt. As a result of the flooding of several lakes the thorny bush surrounding Lamascillindi was transformed into a deep, marshy pool swarming with crocodiles. If Colonel Prigiotti had not been leading the doubats he would certainly—and rightly—have beat a retreat. But he had faith in the white turbans. Fixing rifles and cartridges on their heads the doubats, naked as worms, plunged into the morass and swam across it, beating off the crocodiles, which that day were the allies of the Ethiopians. The garrison of Lamascillindi—supposing itself defended by the morass and its crocodiles—was suddenly awakened by the war-cry of several hundred doubats, rising from the water as if by magic. The battle was short. An hour later the doubats could warm themselves at the flames which devoured the village and destroyed

the fortified outposts built by the Ethiopians round
Lamascillindi. . . .

The battle ended, they learnt that there was another
fortress about ten kilometres away from Lamascillindi.
What was to be done? Return and take another bath
with the crocodiles; go back through the bush? No! . . .
The doubats set off, crushed the Ethiopians and drove
them out of the entire district, and returned that same
day to Dolo.

To sum up: they had covered two hundred and twenty
kilometres on foot, swum in the muddy water, fought
with the crocodiles and gained two battles. And all this
in forty-three hours! . . .

III.—THE MIND OF THE DOUBAT.

There is nothing more difficult and at the same time more
interesting than to penetrate the psychology of more or
less primitive men, hardly touched by civilisation, living in
a world as distant from ours as the constellation of Orion.

With the aid of telescopes we have managed to bridge
the gulf which separates us from distant stars, but nothing
has been invented to elucidate for us the minds of men such
as those who are fighting on the Somalo-Ethiopian frontier.

I have lived with them; I have tried to understand their
acts, their dreams, their desires; I have tried to examine
under an imaginary microscope their soul and their brain.

By citing the doctrines of Freud and Adler, by dwelling
on the researches of Porel and Elisée Reclus, I could em-
bark on long dissertations on the psychology of the doubats.
But not caring much for dissertations, I shall confine
myself to telling some short anecdotes which I collected
in Somaliland, and which throw light on what goes on behind
the ebony faces of the doubats.

*   *   *   *   *

They consider functionaries to be the happiest men in the world, and that work is capable of ennobling no one. They have only a limited confidence in the fidelity of women, whom they treat in a way which would make the most jealous of crusaders shudder with horror. . . .

Intelligent and sceptical, they are rarely taken in, and they are gifted with a developed sense of logic. General Pavone, commander of the Peloritana division, said to his doubats, "We are going to make a great road. Thanks to this road, we shall cover in five hours the same distance which formerly took us ten hours."

The doubats listened attentively to the general's words, then replied,

"That's all very well! But tell us what we are going to do with the extra five hours?"

. . . . .

Uniforms do not impress them. They adored one of their officers who was in the habit of taking sun-baths clad in the scantiest of bathing-costumes. When asked why they preferred this officer to all the others they replied,

"Him naked, him man of the Italian bush. . . ."

. . . . .

One day, on returning to my hut at Bel-Ouen, I discovered that my camp-bed was not made. It was still in the disorder in which I had left it that morning. I summoned the doubat who fulfilled the duties of orderly for me.

"You *bilach*," I said, "why haven't you made my bed?"

"Me no *bilach*," replied the doubat, "me do toukoul, but me not want to touch bed. . . ."

So saying he lifted the pillow, under which I had left my pocket-book.

. . . . .

Asked why he had sent to his village for his four wives, the doubat Ali Youssouf explained to me,

"Me not like them too much. . . . But me like to see and know!"

. . . . .

Sent by Captain D. to Moustahill for the purpose of engaging a cook, the doubat returned alone and reported,

"Me find nothing. All women wives or widows. . . ."

"Well—What of it?"

"Excuse, Captain," cried the doubat, "me not know that wife or widow *do* as cook for you."

. . . . .

The sight of blood makes them literally drunk, and they massacre their enemies mercilessly. They are not, however, cruel. They kill quickly and never make their victims suffer. In short, if one must be killed in Africa it is preferable for the operation to be performed by a doubat, or in general by a Somali. They never think of torturing their enemies as do Ethiopians, Danakils or Issas, whose sadistic cruelty surpasses by far that of the most notorious Chinese executioners. After seeing the atrociously mutilated bodies of little Somali girls and boys, I must say I admire the moderation, control and discipline of the doubats, who content themselves with thrusting their *billao* into the throat of every Ethiopian they come across. It should be added that among all the inhabitants of the East coast of the Dark Continent only the Somalis respect the remains of the fallen foe, which they bury with the same honours that they accord to their own dead.

. . . . .

They carry out their superiors' orders blindly. For example, this is what happened to M. de Martini, Governor-General of Italian Somaliland.

Ships arriving in Somaliland must anchor in the roadstead of Mogadishu, at a distance of about a mile from the port, which cannot be entered owing to the shallows and sharp rocks which make all navigation impossible along the coast. Passengers and goods are landed in small boats that run to and fro between the ships and the port, a difficult enough business, as the sea is always stormy and the roadstead haunted by the sharks that swarm in all parts of the Indian Ocean.

The day on which Governor Martini had to land at Mogadishu the sea was particularly rough.

"We'd better take precautions," said the Prefect as he set off to meet the Governor, who awaited him at the ship's side. So he took with him ten doubats recruited from the best swimmers. Each doubat had a member of the Governor's suite pointed out to him and was given the following order:

"If boat capsizes and white man falls into the sea, you fish him out." . . .

Whereupon they disembarked.

Five hundred metres away from the coast the boat capsized. The Governor and his suite were thrown on the waves. In the course of the salvage work, the doubat who was responsible for M. de Martini's life saw a man—the Governor's doctor—on the point of drowning. Braving wind, water, and sharks, the doubat made for him. After one or two dives, he succeeded in bringing him to the surface. The man clutched desperately on to his rescuer's shoulder. . . . The latter, when he made out the doctor's features, cried, "Oh, but you are not the Mouchir." And threw him back into the sea.

Later when everyone, happily, was saved, the unlucky doctor, who must have passed some ghastly moments, said to the Somali, "Me Mouchir's doctor."

"And me doubat," replied the other proudly, "when we receive order, we carry it out."

And he departed, firmly convinced that he had acted according to the wishes of his superior officer, and that he had fulfilled his duty.

The details did not interest him in the least: he was a doubat.

IV.—ROMANO, SON OF THE DOUBATS.

One day while I was walking along the sandy banks of the Juba, I noticed a young doubat occupied in throwing stones at the crocodiles which, from time to time, showed their disturbing smile on the surface. The sight did not surprise me for crocodiles are as plentiful at Dolo as doubats.

What did surprise me was to see beside the native soldier a little boy, thin and sickly, who wore the uniform of the Lions of Juba, composed of a sort of kilt, a white cloth thrown over the left shoulder, and a white turban. In addition, there hung round his neck the red cord and tassel which distinguish the chiefs from the other doubats. Indeed all the soldiers who passed gave the regulation salute to the little chap, who responded by giving the Roman salute. He was as black as coal.

The mystery of this five-year-old chief intrigued me and I went up to the young doubat and asked,

"Boy belong to you?"

"Yes," replied the doubat, "me boy's father." As he put his long hand on the bony shoulder of the child, he happened to displace the cord, and I saw a little silver cross hanging round the boy's neck.

"You are Christian?"

"Me Mussulman," replied the soldier, "him Christian because him Abyssinian."

"I don't understand you. . . . You are Somali and Mussulman, your son is Abyssinian and Christian. . . . What on earth do you mean?"

"Me his father, as all the doubats and all the officers are his fathers. Real father was Fitaorari Mu-Cria. . . ."

And that was how I made the acquaintance of Romano, son of the doubats.

.   .   .   .   .

When the frontiers between two countries are not defined it is always a very serious matter. When they are defined it can be even more serious.

It is not to be supposed that European countries will submit to surgical operations by commissions, sub-commissions and the other committees charged with the delimitation of frontiers. The red pencils of the areopagi are a long way more dangerous than Jack the Ripper's dagger. In Africa it is the same.

Look at the example of Dolo. This important village —relatively speaking almost a town—was for a long time coveted by both the Italians and the Ethiopians. Situated near the Juba, dominating the Webi-Gestro and Ganale Doria, Dolo is of great strategic importance, and this explains why the town has been for years the object of endless litigation.

At last someone—who very probably has never been to Dolo—had a bright idea. . . . "Dolo must be cut in two," he decided, "half of it must belong to the Italians and the other half to the Ethiopians."

And in the middle of the village they built a wall which defined the frontier between the two countries.

General Pavone commanded the troops of Italian Dolo and the Fitaorari Mu-Cria commanded the troops of Ethiopian Dolo.

FRENZIED WARRIORS HEARING PROCLAMATION OF WAR

FOOD FOR THE HYENAS

British Red Cross Truck on the Dessie Road

War Correspondents at Ease

WITH THE LIONS OF JUBA

The Fitaorari was a brave, simple, likeable and un-prejudiced man. When he was ill, instead of sending for the Coptic monks he called in the Italian doctor, who crossed the frontier with various pills in his pocket and returned with a panther- or leopard-skin over his arm. When he wanted to have the waters of the Juba filtered he visited General Pavone and asked his advice.

One day the General said to him,

"Fitaorari, one of these days I am coming to visit you."

The Fitaorari, who was wise, answered calmly,

"That will be a great honour for me. Only it might happen to be the day of my death."

.   .   .   .   .

Some hours before the attack on Ethiopian Dolo, Italian emissaries were sent to order the Fitaorari Mu-Cria to evacuate the village.

"I am Fitaorari, that is to say the chief of the advance-guard," replied Mu-Cria, "and I shall do my duty . . . every square metre and every toukoul will be defended to our last drop of blood."

A party of Ethiopians had dug themselves into a trench at the entrance to the village, while others barricaded themselves in the toukouls. When the doubats crossed the frontier, the Fitaorari Mu-Cria was standing a few paces from the famous wall.

He is buried on the spot where he died. The Italians, who know how to honour their adversaries, set up some days later a cross on his grave.

.   .   .   .   .

Every toukoul in Dolo had to be taken by force and, as the Fitaorari had predicted, every square metre was taken at the price of blood. Drunk with blood and angered by the resistance of the Ethiopians, the doubats burnt, shot and massacred everywhere they went. They arrived at length in the middle of the village, where Mu-Cria's *ghebi* stood.

They were met by rifle-shots. Two or three of them fell. They attacked with howls, a rain of bullets rattled on the *ghebi*, and a burning torch fell on the straw roof. Forcing the door open, they were brought up short by a young woman with levelled rifle.

She fired three times, then crumpled up, gravely wounded. A child flung himself on her bleeding body. The doubats drew their *billaos* from their sheaths. One of them, holding the child in his left hand, actually raised the right to strike.

He cried out . . . his arm fell. The riding-whip of Doctor Sam had fallen across the doubat's arm, leaving a long red trail from which blood flowed.

. . . . .

Doctor Sambo, who had arrived in Africa on a voluntary service some months since, took in his arms the Fitaorari's wife, while the child scrambled on to the young officer's back and clung to his neck. And while the battle went on, the doctor and his living burden crossed the frontier.

Back in Italian territory, he pulled out several bullets from the woman's body and bound up the dagger-wounds. Then he examined the child and administered a good dose of castor-oil.

Some days later the woman was taken to Mogadishu, where the efforts of the doctors saved her life. When they wanted to take away the child he wept so sorely and clung so desperately to the doctor's tunic that they had to keep him at Dolo.

He received the name of Romano. The doubats, those

same doubats who had been ready to kill him, went to the colonel and said,

"Fitaorari dead. We want to be father to Romano."

They brought him cakes made of *dourah* and crocodiles made of wood. Romano was appointed "Chief of the Band" by the Colonel, and the doubats made him uniforms. A soldier offered him a little camel a few weeks old. A captain had picture-books sent to him from Italy. He sleeps in Doctor Sambo's tent, gives the Roman salute and eats in the officer's mess. He is happy. Sometimes he passes a little wooden cross which stands at the foot of the frontier-wall, and goes on playing and laughing, heedless.

He is only five: he knows nothing.

.   .   .   .   .

Romano suffers from a serious disease of the liver. The doctors told me that if he had gone on living with his parents he would have been dead in a few years. Under the care of Doctor Sambo, he will be cured.

How strange life is! The Fitaorari Mu-Cria thought he died for the Negus and for his country: he was sacrificed simply to save the life of his son!

Unhappily he will never know it. YES, HE DOES KNOW.

V.—STRONGHOLDS OF THE DOUBATS.

From Malcar-rei, where the frontiers of Ethiopia, Kenya and Italian Somaliland meet, as far as the plains of Ogaden, a long line of fortifications stretches out through the bush. Of all sizes, of all colours.

The fortress of Malcar-rei, designed to protect the ferry which assures communication between the two banks, is constructed of tree-trunks covered with pitch. The one at Tejiglo, of red brick, seems to flame in the rays of the African sun. The fort at Moustahill, called "Fitaorari," that is to say, "Chief of the Advance-guard," is pure white, and with its heavy blocks of stone looks like the forts one sees in Morocco. I have even seen a green fortress: that of Ouladdei, made of wood, steel wire, creepers and thorny acacia whose branches and leaves almost entirely cover the primitive construction.

Whether they are made of wood, dressed cement, granite, acacia or cocoa-tree leaves, the fortifications shelter a good number of doubats, some white officers, half-a-dozen machine-guns, some twenty camels or mules, and finally a well. I nearly forgot the most important thing: each fort contains a heliograph.

The heliograph resembles a huge tortoise turned over and hoisted to the top of an iron structure. Under the tortoise all sorts of cranks, wheels, and mysterious chains, all with names of Greco-Latin origin which make one think of the Pharaohs. The names are unimportant. What matters is that, thanks to the glass tortoise, fortresses can communicate with one another by throwing out beams of blinding light into the tropical darkness. During the day they work it in the same way by using the rays of the sun, caught by the receiver with the aid of huge mirrors. In this way they manage to transmit important messages.

Among the bush-fortresses which I visited in the course of my journey along the Somali front, the most interesting is the one at Dagnerrei, situated between Callafo and Bour-Dodi, near the Webbe-Shibeli river. Dagnerrei, one of the most important outposts of the Ethiopian army, was defended by the troops of Fitaorari Ato Becha. Attacked by the doubats of Commander Fava and the followers of Ol-Ol Dinlé, sultan of the Scavellis, Ato Becha fled, after a desperate resistance. It was during the siege of Dagnerrei that the doubats demanded to attack it in the most dangerous quarter, as I have already described.

WITH THE LIONS OF JUBA

Two weeks after the departure of Ato Becha, I lunched in the tent which he had occupied. Thanks to fourteen days uninterrupted cleansing, we could stay there for half-an-hour without being asphyxiated.

I have held in my hand his journal of the fort, a thick book bound in cloth labelled as follows: "Specially made for G. M. Mohamedally & Co., Jijiga." In *Ghez* writing, Ato Becha had day by day noted down the events, and concluded by this laconic phrase: "The fort will be taken in several hours. I am retiring. . . ."

And he retired, in company with Hamel Badil, a well-known Ethiopian. His men went on fighting. When the fortress was taken, and Lieutenant Paterno hoisted the Tricolour over Ato Becha's toukoul, the struggle continued on the hills and rocks round Dagnerrei. Finally the Ethiopians—after a hand-to-hand fight in the bush which lasted over a quarter-of-an-hour—beat a retreat and disappeared in the forests of Webbe-Shibeli, taking with them their wounded. But not the dead. Next day when the breaches had been filled up, the barbed wire reinforced and the machine-guns replaced—not to speak of the heliograph—the doubats searched the caves, the precipices, and the bush.

After rendering them military honours, they buried them in a common grave near the fort, doubats and Ethiopians.

They thought they had found all the dead. . . . They were wrong.

The Webbe-Shibeli, being one of the richest rivers for crocodile and hippopotamus, I went out one afternoon with a rifle to lie in wait for the beasts. I saw no hippopotami, but I was astounded at the number of crocodiles. After waiting a good half-hour for one of the reptiles to leave the water and settle down in the sand, I saw one about three or four hundred metres away getting ready to

149

take its *siesta*. In order to approach it I plunged into some very dense bush, but before I had covered a hundred metres I had to stop. An atrocious smell poisoned the atmosphere.

Hiding my face in my handkerchief, I went on, expecting to find some animal's carcase.

I stood petrified with disgust and horror. . . . It was a man's body, half-eaten by hyenas. . . .

A skull whitened by the sun and a leg in a khaki gaiter. . . . That was all that was left of the man fallen before Dagnerrei. He had died very probably a little way off, in a cave or perhaps at the bottom of the trenches. The hyenas must have dragged his body as far as the banks of the Webbe-Shibeli. What was his name? Where did he come from? No matter . . . human life counts so little in Somaliland.

A hundred paces further on I found two more corpses. Forgetting the crocodile hunt, I began to run. I informed the commander of a little Italian post about a kilometre from the river, and an hour later the flames of a vast bon-fire consumed the remains of the three men reclaimed by the bush.

One of the doubats, while building the bonfire, found a spear which had belonged to one of the Ethiopians, and took possession of the trophy. When the dry branches of the burning bed began to crackle, he took the spear and went off in the direction of the camp.

Before he had gone very far he changed his mind and retraced his steps. He went to the place where the three Ethiopians had fallen, and stuck the spear in the ground. Then, bowing low, he seemed to murmur a prayer.

Then he took his rifle and rejoined the other doubats who sang as they left the bonfire, whose acrid smoke hung heavily over the bush.

VI.—THE MEN ON MULES.

"You will be impaled for five hours," said the man on the mule to the doubat, "for having contradicted and insulted the yousbashi."

"Ferid, very good," replied the doubat, standing correctly to attention.

Then he added, "All the same, I was right."

.   .   .   .   .

In the Somali bush one often meets bands of doubats, marching with rapid strides and singing the savage and monotonous songs of their country. In the middle of the bronze warriors prances the white officer: the man on a mule.

Remaining in the saddle for ten or more hours a day, attacking enemy fortresses, camping in the bush, going for weeks without presentable food, swallowing great doses of the red dust of Africa, leading the life of wandering fighters —all that is relatively easy. What is much more difficult is to maintain authority by inspiring the respect of those splendid barbarians the doubats.

The smallest injustice committed on a native, the slightest gesture betraying impatience, nervousness or fear, an involuntary word capable of wounding their religious feelings is sufficient to turn the love and respect which they feel for their officers into a dangerous insubordination, sometimes hate.

Doubtless the men in white turbans are big children, but children armed with Mannlicher rifles and a hundred-and-fifty cartridges!

The mule-riders must be severe beyond a doubt, and also just. Then the doubats love them. Moreover they should be married and religious. Then they are respected.

"You have *nag* (wife) at home, Captain?"

It is invariably the first question the doubats ask an officer when they get to know him.

If the reply is in the affirmative they are content. If it is in the negative, the rumour goes round: "Him no *nag*, him *bilach*."

If the officer is not married he will have to give evidence of a good many other qualities to excuse this terrible short-coming.

"Colonello has no *nag*, but you like him don't you?" I asked one of the doubats of Colonel Carnevali, commander of the regiment of Fer-Fer.

"Him no *nag*," replied the doubat, "but him eat with us, him eat much, and him kill many Abyssinians."

When the chaplains celebrate mass, the doubats—who are without exception Moslems or fetichists—prowl round the place to see if all the officers are fulfilling their religious duties. They tell in Somaliland the story of a young Israelite officer who attends mass regularly every Sunday to avoid being treated as a "*bilach*" man. The doubats sometimes pardon injustice, often celibacy, but never lack of belief or piety.

Although the white leaders of the doubats have to face countless difficulties and pass many tests to keep the esteem and respect of their soldiers, the ambition of everyone fighting in Somaliland is to become "mule-riders," that is to say leaders of the doubats.

It is not easy to obtain this position. The selection is perhaps the more careful because it means being attached to the staff. Courage and strength of mind are not enough. It is necessary to know the country, or at least Africa, that continent still full of secrets, full of mysteries, full of surprises. One must know the primitive and at the same time enigmatic heart of the inhabitants of this strange country, ravaged by revolts, raids, punitive expeditions, wars and internal strife. One must in fact know everything there is to be known about African warfare, of war in the bush. One must be able to fight with unflagging energy against guerilla tactics, dust, wild beasts, tse-tse flies and enemy agents who come and go, slipping out to disappear in the equatorial night. . . .

Most of the officers who command the doubats are men who—like Prigiotti or Carnevali—have fought in every corner of Africa where the Tricolour flies. They pursued Omar el Mouktar in the Cyrenian desert, they faced the hordes of the Mullah, "The poor man of God," on the sandy banks of the River of Leopards; they crushed the warriors of Abscir Dorré in the Ogaden bush; they spilt their blood on the white walls of El-bour or Benadir, fighting the fierce mercenaries of Omar Samantar. They are men who would die of boredom and despair if they were obliged to sleep in a real bed, eat anything else but preserved food, or if Africa, all Africa, was finally pacified.

. . . . . .

I spoke to a doubat who was "impaled." . . . Do not think that the officers of the doubats want to rival certain *seraskiers* of the Sublime Porte or certain Moldavian roivodes. Far from it! . . . To be "impaled" is the lightest punishment they inflict on the doubats. It means that the culprit is lashed to a picket and kept there for several hours. Obviously not pleasant considering the strength of the African sun. But the doubats prefer it to punishment number two, only applied in serious cases.

This punishment, dreaded most of all by the doubats, is really terrible: half-pay for two weeks, involving the loss of thirty-five lira.

"Impale me for ten hours, but don't keep back my pay!" say the doubats to the officer who is punishing them.

If they perceive any hesitation, they never fail to add, "Don't forget, Captain, that you are my father and mother."

VII.—THE CONDOTTIERE OF THE BUSH.

If Ol-Ol Dinlé, Sultan of the Sciavelli, were to fight with English troops in some forgotten corner of the Empire, he would be respected and admired, and Fleet Street would publish his biography.

If Ol-Ol Dinlé were to fight with French troops, after a while he would be decorated.

But neither English nor French would understand, even while honouring it, the enigmatic mind of this strange warrior from the savage land of the Sciavelli, who became in a few years the most famous man in all East Africa.

But the Italians, *they* are capable of understanding this type of man. For Ol-Ol Dinlé, sultan of the bush, is related to their ancestors. Is he not in reality extraordinarily like the *Condottiere*, an African rival of the Sforza, the Forte-braccio, the Giussano or the Colleoni? Though we are four centuries and 4,000 kilometres from the Renaissance and Italy, Ol-Ol Dinlé belongs to the time and the country which saw the flowering of the most bizarre lives, which witnessed the most fabulous adventures, and which, pardoning cruelty and esteeming courage in oneself, without discriminating between good and evil, could appreciate the men who were content to live under their own star.

. . . . .

The Sciavelli inhabit the territories bordering on Somaliland and Ethiopia, between Fer-Fer and Callafo. The land belongs to the family of Ol-Ol Dinlé whose wealth is legendary. In a country where the possession of ten cows represents a fortune, in a country where for the loss of five dromedaries you can obtain a beautiful wife—for the women here are beautiful—the family of Ol-Ol Dinlé possesses herds consisting of nearly twenty thousand head of cattle. In short, if Ol-Ol Dinlé is the *Condottiere* of the bush, his family is something which corresponds to the synthetic and symbolical house of Rothschild.

Thus it was with no idea of enriching himself that Ol-Ol Dinlé, the black sultan, set an army of followers on the march from the moment of the first rifle-shots in Ogaden. For him it was first and foremost a question of settling accounts. Some decades ago the Ethiopians did Ol-Ol Dinlé's father a bad turn. Taken prisoner during a frontier skirmish, the sultan's father was led into the interior of Abyssinia. After a long captivity he suffered the same treatment which was meted out to the famous Ras Hailu. The arms and legs of the prisoner are squeezed between tree-trunks with cords attached to their ends. Then the cords are twisted, and this action eventually causes the improvised leggings to break the prisoner's bones. If the tortured man survives, they have a way of "finishing off" which never fails. They squeeze the wretch's chest between the same tree-trunks, work the cords in the same way, and the chest, and life with it, is utterly crushed.

Ol-Ol Dinlé's father being executed in this way, one can easily imagine that the sultan has not much love for his neighbours, the Ethiopians. Nor does he feel very tenderly towards the members of his family who, the moment war actually broke out, ranged themselves on the side of his enemies. Among these black sheep of the *kabyla* of the Sciavelli, is one whom the sultan of the bush particularly hates. This is Hamel Badil, whose history is worth recording.

· · · · · ·

During the siege of Dagnerrei, Commander Fava's troops were strongly supported by Ol-Ol Dinlé's followers who by occupying the hills and mountains in the environs of Dagnerrei made it impossible for relief expeditions to approach. The sultan, after joining in the attack of the stronghold, managed with several hundreds of his men to cut off the retreat of the Ethiopians who were transporting their wounded in the direction of Northern Ogaden. Among these fugitives was Hamel Badil.

Hamel Badil was Ol-Ol Dinlé's own cousin. Full of ambition, courage and astuteness, he dreamed of becoming sultan and laying his hand on his cousin's fortune. He enlisted in the Ethiopian army and the Negus gave him the command of the Dagnerrei district. The day they brought the news to Ol-Ol Dinlé, he said harshly,

"Now one of us must disappear."

Knowing that Ol-Ol Dinlé and his forces were camped in the district, Hamel Badil, after the fall of Dagnerrei, had no illusions as to the fate that awaited him.

"I am fleeing because you are too powerful," he wrote in a letter addressed to Commander Fava on the day after the occupation of Dagnerrei, "but I send you my wife and my two children. Protect them and God will bless you. As for me, I am in the hands of Allah. . . ."

When the letter arrived at its destination Hamel Badil was no longer in the hands of Allah, but in those of the Sciavelli. Ol-Ol Dinlé reserved for his cousin the most respectful welcome, due to a prince of the blood. He had a sumptuous tent pitched for him, sent him the best dishes that native cooks could prepare, and, last but not least, put at his relation's disposal the most beautiful flowers of his harem. When night descended on the banks of the Webbe-Shibeli, he had Hamel Badil, the man who had to disappear, strangled in cold blood.

That the story might be even more typical of an episode in the Renaissance, the delicate operation was confided to Hamel Badil's own brother who was at that time in Ol-Ol Dinlé's camp.

.   .   .   .   .

A strange person, the sultan of the Sciavelli. Lean, bony, silent as a monk or a hermit. A few days after the execution of his cousin he threw himself into the Webbe-Shibeli and braving the undesirable reptiles that wallow in it, saved the life of one of his followers who was on the point of drowning. Forty-eight hours later they shot at his order the same man, accused of selling cartridges to the Ethiopians.

Rival of the famous mullah, extraordinary mixture of soldier and prophet, bandit and hero, this sultan of the bush, this black *Condottiere*, faces death as if it was the most insignificant thing in the world. In every battle he is the first to make an onslaught on the enemy trenches. To save two dromedaries he is ready to risk his skin and sacrifice the lives of a hundred men. One sees him weeping on the tomb of one of his children, dead at an early age, and one sees him witness, without betraying the slightest emotion, the execution of a dozen of his men accused of treason. Mounted on horseback, he casts an indifferent eye on the ghastly sight presented by the burning or despoiling of a town or village. But when night falls, and the voice of the muezzin is heard from the minarets, Ol-Ol Dinlé prostrates himself in the direction of the sacred stone of Kaaba, murmuring prayers full of pious humility.

A few days after my arrival in the stronghold of Fitaorari, Ol-Ol Dinlé—encamped in the vicinity of Calafo—came to receive orders from General Graziani. To reach the fortress a steep hill has to be climbed, bordered by a precipice fifty

metres deep. Down to the bottom of this precipice fell
the sultan's car, driven by an unwary chauffeur. All the
occupants were seriously hurt with the exception of Ol-Ol
Dinlé, who after recovering consciousness in the car, smashed
like an egg, scrambled up the precipice without help, and
reached the fortress on foot so as to inform the Italians.

"It was lucky you weren't killed," said one of the officers
to the sultan, some hours later.

"Luck?" replied the Somali proudly, "I have none of
that. . . . It is destiny and the will of God which reserves
me for a more glorious end than dying in a ravine!"

His men adore him and consider him as a sort of divinity.
His enemies cherish a deadly hate for him, and compare
him to the most evil spirits. Bad or good, God or Devil,
bandit of legendary hero, this sultan of the bush is undoubtedly a warrior. . . . And, as Marshal Lyautey once
said, "One does not colonize with young girls."

Ol-Ol Dinlé, sultan of the Sciavelli, is certainly not a
young girl!

VIII.—THE WOMEN OF THE DOUBATS.

Ten or twenty kilometres from the front lines and
fortifications, where the supply bases of the Italians are,
one invariably sees a sort of encampment surrounded with a
a strong iron fence.

"A prisoners' camp?" I asked on seeing for the first time
the collection of little toukouls.

The officer who was with me replied smiling, "Not
exactly. They are the dwelling-huts of the doubats and
the Askaris' wives."

"That's very interesting," I said. "Let's go and see
them."

"Sorry! . . . But orders are orders. . . . You can
visit and photograph everything you want. I even authorise

you to make sketches of the forts and examine the guns. We have no secrets. . . . As for the women, it is forbidden for anyone with a white skin to enter the encampment. . . . The doubats' women are 'taboo.'"

Just then one of them passed, carrying a clay pot filled with water. She disappeared behind the railings. For the first time in my life I regretted that I was not a native.

. . . . .

Jealousy is born in men, be they civilized or savage.

After seeing their women, one can understand that the doubats are no exception to this rule.

I do not think another country exists where, proportionately speaking, one meets so many pretty women as in the Somali bush. In the smallest village one sees at least a dozen women each of whom is beautiful enough to be the envy of the vamps of Hollywood. Tall, slim, long-legged, with velvety skin, sparkling eyes, fine limbs and perfect figures, usually swathed in silk stuffs, these women are unusually beautiful.

It must be added that, though the colour of their skin is the same as the other inhabitants of the black continent, the Somalis, whose ancestors came very probably from Yemen, have not at all negroid characteristics. No fleshy hanging lips, no thick nose. The difference of race shows itself equally in their bearing and manners. The blood of Arab conquerors runs in the veins of the Somali.

. . . . .

The Mohammedan religion has two great merits. It has inspired the architecture of Islam. It has established the life of the women in such a way that it remains after centuries an absorbing subject for study.

In this respect Somaliland holds the greatest surprises

for the traveller. First of all, contrary to the custom of Eastern or Southern countries inhabited by Moslems, Somali women do not wear the veil. It is true that against possible dangers the Somalis take other precautions far more effective than a little piece of transparent silk.

Another surprise. No harems, no *zenanas*, no armed guardians, no palaces or hermetically sealed quarters. The Somali woman is not a slave; she is free, or relatively so. Certainly she has not the right to vote in the councils, but she can work, walk about, rest, and amuse herself as she pleases. In Somaliland one would search in vain for the iron discipline, and heavy atmosphere of the Oriental harem. Nothing but a family life, simple, calm, well-balanced.

Each man has four wives.

. . . . .

In most primitive countries, the young man who is love-stricken and wants to marry has to buy his woman by addressing himself to her father.

In Somali this is not the case. Before entering into negotiations with his future father-in-law, the man must consult the girl. She has the right to say "yes."

If she says no, the man can address himself to her father who, being usually a man of age and experience, knows the most likely ways of making a young woman change her mind. The violent contact of the skin with a bamboo-rod being more than disagreeable, the girl ends by giving her consent.

The beauty, health, intelligence or manners of a girl have nothing to do with the price which her husband pays for her. It is only the *kabyla*, that is to say pedigree, which counts. The Bimal being former slaves, the price of a woman belonging to that tribe does not exceed five camels. On the contrary, in the Migourtina some tribes estimate the

ITALIAN CONSUL OF GONDAR LEAVES ABYSSINIA

ABYSSINIAN SAMARITANS

value of a woman at anything up to hundred dromedaries. The price of one of these beasts being about five hundred francs, one may say that in certain parts of Somaliland women are priceless. The price was justified when the Somali were given to cannibalism, and could at a pinch eat their wives. To-day, at a time of crisis, it is a bit expensive.

The institution of divorce exists in this country. A judgment of separation is delivered by the *Cadi* of the tribe. The numbers of explorers from the United States—and consequently the American influence—being very limited, in a case of divorce the man is not obliged to pay a pension of dromedaries or coco-nuts to his ex-partner.

.   .   .   .   .   .

Between battles the doubats come back to their wives. When night falls they light a great bonfire in the middle of the encampment, and in the flickering light of the flames, to the sound of a primitive instrument made of some bits of iron, the doubats dance. The women, seated round the fire, lift up their soft voices, and mark the rhythm by beating with their nervous hands the drums made of goat-skin. The rhythm of the songs and the dance becomes more and more rapid, the gestures more and more savage, cries well up from the throats of the dancers with increasing ferocity. From time to time shots ring out and red flames sear the deep blue of the tropical night. The doubats are amusing themselves.

They only regret that they are among their own people: they cannot kill anyone.

IX.—THE DOUBAT AND DEATH.

I have not delved far enough into medical literature to know if anyone has ever gone into the question of the relative power of resistance to death of different races.

If researches of this nature have never been undertaken, I would urge any scientists who might be interested in this problem to go to Somaliland, where a considerable number of subjects for study are to be found.

The Somalis, who seem to be practically insensible to physical pain, survive injuries which would kill the strongest men of another country.

At the hospital in Dolo, Doctor Sambo showed me a doubat who was eating his dinner with an obvious appetite.

One evening he had arrived at the hospital, got down from his camel, and showed himself to the doctor.

"Me a little sick," he said.

The doctor examined him, took the bandage off his chest, then called the other doctors to have a look at the "miracle." . . . The doubat's right lung was perforated by a bullet.

"When were you wounded?" asked the doctor.

"This morning," replied the patient. "Me take camel and come here at once. But not able to come quick."

"To-day," said the doctor, "he is almost cured."

I have told the story of the doubat who attacked a machine-gun unaided. It is a fact that at the moment he overpowered the last machine-gunner with his *billao* he had six bullets in his chest. Neither more nor less. Before dying he summoned enough force to kill a man.

At the hospital of Fer-Fer, I was present at an operation on a doubat. They had to take out three ribs. As the patient suffered from heart-disease they could not put him to sleep. At the moment when the doctor plunged his knife into the man's flesh I expected horrible shrieks. Not a murmur. . . . Very pale and trembling, the sick man clutched the edge of the table, fixing his eye on the roof of the tent. He underwent the entire operation without uttering a cry.

Another day I met an old Askari who had taken part in the battle of Adowa. He had the misfortune to fall into the hands of the Ethiopians, who are not more tender towards the Askaris than the Askaris are towards the Ethiopians!

They had cut off his right hand and his left foot. Describing this ghastly night of blood-shed, he said,

". . . Then I recovered consciousness. I dragged myself to some bushes. I got some dry branches together, and making a fire, I inserted a little bit of wood into my veins, and put my mutilated arm and foot into the flames. . . . Thus I did not lose too much blood, and survived from my wounds. . . ."

Another instance. . . . One evening, to get back from Genalie to Mogadishio, they had the impertinence to put at my disposal a native chauffeur whose eye was no better than his hearing, and who seemed afflicted with megalomania. Evidently he took himself for Sir Malcolm Campbell and thought that the road between Afgoi and Mogadishio was to be compared with the famous track on Daytona beach. We had to implore our chauffeur to be content for once with a speed of sixty miles an hour. In short, after nearly crashing into military lorries half-a-dozen times, he ended by running over a native who was going patiently towards his village with his camel. This is what I found on examining the man as he lay on the road: both legs, an arm, a rib and a collar-bone broken, the spinal column injured, wounds in the neck and the abdomen. If my friend Sosthénes de la Rochefoucauld—who could be my witness— had not been with me I would not dare to assert this: that the man had not lost consciousness, and that at the hospital in Mogadishio, when they put him on the operation-table, he sat up and tried to keep off the surgeons. . . .

All the same, that did not keep him from dying some hours later.

It is difficult to kill them . . . but when the hour of their end comes they make no fuss.

Watching them face death with so much courage, I would even say with so much serenity, I thought that they were insensible to pain and suffering, as to annihilation. I was mistaken. I discovered it on the night when my servant Ibrahim the doubat, the same who killed his wife and her friend, had to go out with a small detachment to attack an Ethiopian position. The doubat smelt blood. He seemed happy. Seated in front of my tent in the tropical night, I awaited the sound of the trumpet summoning him to the fort from which he would leave for the bush.

"You're happy, aren't you?" I said to Ibrahim. "You never think that you may die?" . . .

"I think of it often, General," replied the doubat, "but I am not afraid of death. . . . Do you know the Koran? When I cross the bridge of Alshirath I shall be much happier than on this earth. I shall live in the shade of perfumed trees and drink nectar, and a hundred houris, of whom the ugliest is as beautiful as the sun will dance round me. . . . So I shall pass my days in eternity."

The sound of the trumpet tore the silence. Ibrahim took his rifle and stuck his *billao* in his belt.

"May Allah the all-powerful bless you!" he said.

Footsteps echoed. White shadows arose. The whinnying of camels mingled with the harsh voices of the doubats.

And Ibrahim the doubat, who believed in the perfumed trees, the nectar and the houris of the Beyond, bowed for the last time before me and left content, with a light heart and a smile on his lips. . . .

UNDER FIRE WITH THE EMPEROR

By STUART EMENY

*War-Correspondent to the "News-Chronicle"
with the Abyssinian Army in Dessie*

UNDER FIRE WITH THE EMPEROR

IT was on a wild, wet night in August that I arrived in Addis Ababa.

For two days I had jogged along in the train which climbs up Abyssinia's one and only single track railway from the festering heat of Djibouti (Red Sea Port in French Somaliland) to Addis Ababa, the mountain Capital of Haile Selassie, King of Kings and Conquering Lion of Judah.

My travelling companions had been Evelyn Waugh, the novelist, two cinema news-reel photographers, and Mr. F. W. Rickett, who in a few days was to startle the world and embarrass the British diplomats by coolly announcing that he had purchased a concession to exploit oil and minerals throughout half Abyssinia—half the territory which Mussolini coveted.

While even then we regarded Ricketts as "a mystery man" and did not think that his story of bringing funds from the Coptic Church of the Near East to the Coptic Church of Abyssinia for the Red Cross was the whole reason for his visit, we never dreamed of the sensation he was to cause within the next few days.

Certainly "big business" did not weigh heavily on Rickett's shoulders. He had all the carefree gaiety of a schoolboy on a spree.

It was teeming with rain when we finally jettisoned at 8.30 in the evening on to the dimly lit platform at Addis Ababa, amid a herd of Abyssinians in dirty white chammas—the toga-like national costume—Indians, and European hotel proprietors of many nationalities all touting for our custom.

A last, lingering look at the two-coach train which seemed to be the final link with civilisation, and I braced myself to the horrors of Addis Ababa and Abyssinia, which had been painted so vividly in everything I had read about the country. The thought of one's medicine chest, mosquito net, and portable bath were consoling. Then to my surprise I found myself shepherded into a taxi which put its London counterpart to shame, and a few minutes later was shown into the electric glare of an hotel lounge.

Even more surprising was the excellent dinner served and the fact that every bedroom had a spacious bathroom with h. and c. running water. I did not then realise that this was the one building in the whole of Ethiopia with proper bathrooms and that they only existed there because the hotel was built beside a hot spring. Here I later found the élite of the Legations came, with slightly shamefaced air, to take their "weekly!" tub.

After dinner I was taken in a balloon-tyred limousine taxi to see the night life of Addis. We looked in at a couple of the capital's three cinemas and saw a news reel of the previous year's Boat Race and Greta Garbo talking French in a "six reel" melodrama. All the sound tracks of talkies were in French, the second language of the country; and because no cinema had more than one projector films had to be shown in the old fashioned method, with the consequent intervals for changing the reels. The night clubs, with their shaded lights, cramped dance floors, and clients making whoopee in a rather depressing sort of way, had much the same dismal atmosphere of misfired gaiety as their London counterparts.

The following morning I saw Addis Ababa as a strange city of contrasts, with its extraordinary mixture of African and Western civilisation, in which the Middle Ages and the twentieth century seemed to rub shoulders.

UNDER FIRE WITH THE EMPEROR

Shops and cinemas of stone European construction stood side by side with wood frame and mud-walled shacks and native "tukuls," which looked like, and, indeed, were little better than hollow haystacks. Delicatessen shops, which sold caviar, overlooked the native market, where grain, dried peas, and red pepper, which form the main part of the natives' diet, were stacked in basket trays on the muddy ground. Motors driven by reckless Abyssinian chauffeurs rushed through throngs of pack mules, horses, donkeys and occasional camels which straggled all over the roads. A khaki-topeed policeman attempted to direct traffic at the main cross roads, and every few days the Minister of the Interior sent out his minions to teach the population road-sense with a whip.

When I arrived preparations for the inevitable war were in full swing. From dawn to dusk recruits were drilling in the streets, forming fours, squelching barefoot through the mud, and as often as not presenting arms with their rifles upside down. The story was told among the journalists that the N.C.O. used to drill his men every morning in a wood outside Addis while a tribe of baboons looked on from the trees. One morning the officer arrived before his men to find all the baboons lined up drilling with sticks on their shoulders!

Day by day the drum and fife band of the Imperial Guard, led by its seven foot tall drum major (who was executed by the Italians after the capture of Addis), marched round the streets playing patriotic tunes to collect recruits, as if in parody of the recruiting days in London in 1914-15. Mule caravans of ammunition trailed off to replenish the arsenals of the Rases on the frontiers. Air raid precaution measures were published, and scared the population so much that many natives fled the town while scores of Greeks, Armenians, and Indians sold up their businesses and left the country.

ABYSSINIAN STOP PRESS

This started a run on the bank for foreign currency and caused the thaler—the Maria Theresa dollar of the currency—to fall for several weeks to unheard of low levels. In the early hours troop trains steamed out of Addis. A bugle would sound and from the back streets and hutments warriors would leave weeping women for the station. Each man wore a couple of bandoliers of treasured cartridges and carried a small sack containing enough grain and dried meat to last him for a month. Some carried modern rifles, but many had guns which had been used at the first battle of Adowa 40 years previously.

The faith of Abyssinia in the League of Nations and in the belief that Great Britain, in particular, would come to her assistance was pathetic. Equally touching was the belief of everybody from Government officials to the Ethiopian man in the street that if necessary they could thrash the Italians single-handed. They seemed incapable of appreciating the overwhelming strength of a modern Great Power equipped with mechanised transport, tanks, aeroplanes, poison gas and unlimited ammunition. The Abyssinian Press, which consists of several Government-controlled newspapers, in which the Emperor occasionally wrote the editorials, began at this stage to reflect these sentiments. Up till then the Ethiopian papers had shown praiseworthy restraint, and one editor who had said something uncomplimentary about the Italians had been put into chains.

It was in this atmosphere of impending war that over a hundred journalists, photographers and cinema men found themselves. They crowded themselves into the hotels where the proprietors immediately doubled their prices. The Ethiopian Government was completely nonplussed as to how to deal with the Press. A Press Bureau, it is true, was opened, but it was of little use to the journalists as it confined itself almost entirely to the issuing of the briefest and most uninteresting of communiques.

Fired with ambition to go to the front as soon as war broke out the Press equipped itself with "caravans." Mules, tents, camping gear of every kind was purchased and *nagadis* (mule boys) were hired. Journalists dressed themselves in the weirdest assortment of costumes some of them looking like a cross between a cowboy and a relic of the Boer War. Elaborate rehearsals were held in the grounds of the hotels, where tents were pitched and grown men played at camping.

On my eighth day in Addis I was awakened at about 4 o'clock one morning by a loud hammering on my bedroom door. Staggering sleepily out of bed I opened the door to find Mr. Rickett standing there.

"It's signed and sealed!" he gasped. "Lend me an electric torch."

I was much too sleepy to care what had been signed and sealed but I lent him the torch and he disappeared into the darkness.

When I saw him later that morning as he was packing up to rush off to Europe he told me of the enormous concession he had purchased from the Emperor.

The concession was granted at a time when Mr. Eden was moralising to Italy and it was inevitable the British Government should be accused of being behind the deal. As a matter of fact nobody was more surprised than the British Government when the news was published and the British Legation in Addis Ababa was positively dumbfounded.

The Ethiopian Government by granting the concession embarrassed its most powerful champion which was Great Britain and made her suspect in the eyes of the world. It was the Emperor's one diplomatic mistake.

ABYSSINIAN STOP PRESS

The Emperor insisted on meeting every European who arrived in his capital and the journalists were not exempt. The interview was something of an ordeal. When my turn came I was shown into a large reception room, almost entirely devoid of furniture. At the far end of the room, some thirty yards away, the Emperor sat at a large, bare table with his back to a huge window. The Emperor rose as I walked the length of the room towards him. He was wearing a long black silk cloak and white jodphurs. After shaking hands he motioned me to a chair some ten feet away and directly opposite him so that the full light from the window fell on my face while he remained a mere silhouette —an interviewing trick which the Emperor had apparently borrowed from Mussolini.

An embarrassing silence followed. The Emperor did not speak and I did not know whether it was the correct thing to speak first in a royal presence. When nothing had been said for some thirty seconds I ventured to introduce myself and to explain the policy of the paper I represented.

The Emperor solemnly replied: "Yes, I know that the *News Chronicle* is a very serious paper." Another long silence. For want of polite drawing-room conversation with royalty I explained the state of public opinion in England and the attitude of the Press generally with regard to the impending conflict.

The Emperor expressed the opinion that the Press of the world was interpreting Abyssinia's case with extraordinary fairness. Unable to stand another period of silence I rose, bowed, and sidled from the room with as much dignity as possible.

A week or so later the Emperor gave a banquet to the entire Press in the modern palace he had had built five years previously for his coronation. The banquet was held in a long corridor and the table was laid with gold plate and decorated with the colours of Ethiopia in flowers. No raw meat feast this, but a well served and well cooked European meal from hors d'oeuvre to dessert, with all the appropriate wines. Fuzzie-headed Abyssinian flunkeys in bottle-green tailed coats, red knee-breeches and white stockings danced attendance.

The only diversion was an intermittent failure of the electric lights. Apparently the royal electrician, anxious to show the palace illuminations at their best had over-charged the wiring system with the result that the fuses were blown every few minutes. Every time the banquet was plunged into darkness footmen rushed in with hurricane lamps.

In view of the imminence of war the Maskal ceremony of September 27, which commemorates at once the finding of the True Cross and the end of the rainy season in Abyssinia, took on a special significance. This year the end of the rains meant that Italy would now be able to launch the attack. The rains are supposed to cease at two o'clock in the afternoon promptly, but this year a torrential storm broke over the great military parade staged before the Emperor. But despite the rain thousands of warriors, wearing lions' mane head-dresses and carrying gold and silver--embossed rhinoceros shields, paid homage to the Emperor and mimed to him how they would fight the enemy.

"We will fight like lions," shouted one chief, brandishing his sword.

"We will dig the Italians out of their trenches and drive them into the sea."

The Abyssinians conveniently found that the fact that it had rained at the Maskal ceremony was a good omen, while the Italian native levies in Eritrea who were holding their own ceremony found it an auspicious portent that the smoke from the Maskal bonfires drifted towards Abyssinia. So everybody was satisfied.

A couple of days later news came that Italian troops had moved from their base at Asmara in Eritrea down to the Abyssinian frontier. The Emperor, who so far had deliberately delayed giving the general mobilisation order (although it was actually printed) as he did not wish to prejudice any chance of last-minute peace negotiations, decided that he could delay no longer. Journalists and photographers were informed that the great war drum, which signified the Call to Arms in Abyssinia, would be beaten on October 3. The whole show was to be stage-managed for the benefit of the Press but even the Ethiopian court officials who were the stage managers could not foresee the impromptu drama in which the ceremony was to end.

On the appointed day journalists and camera men were marshalled on a terrace inside the ancient palace of the Emperor Menelik—the White Hall of Ethiopia—while in a courtyard below them were some 5,000 of Abyssinia's most savage looking warriors. The war drum began to beat. The Minister of the Pen started to read a long proclamation explaining that the Emperor had done everything in his power to avoid war and ending with an appeal to the manhood of Ethiopia to rally to the colours now that war was imminent.

As the proclamation was being read the crowd of warriors below became more and more excited, shouting battle cries, waving spears and rifles, gashing their own foreheads with their swords, and gradually pressing forward towards the terrace. Suddenly the whole mob charged and rushed the terrace steps on which the journalists and other European visitors were gathered. Taken by surprise and fearing that this was the start of a massacre of the whites the whole of the Europeans turned and fled. I saw one photographer slip on the steps.

As the horde of frenzied warriors swept forward I saw

one ruffian who had blood gushing from his forehead grab
the photographer by the scruff of the neck and carry him
bodily on to the terrace. Court officials waving staves rushed
forward and drove the warriors back. And in the midst of
all this confusion a messenger rushed in with a telegram
stating that that morning Italian 'planes had bombed
Adowa and that the Italian invasion of Abyssinia had
started.

Journalists raced for their cars, typing the news as they
sped to the wireless station. Within half an hour the radio
was jammed with "copy" and the Government imposed a
200-word limit on further cables.

Anti-aircraft guns appeared in the main streets of the
city and we all went to bed that night fully expecting to be
bombed at dawn. Numbers of European traders packed
their goods on to motor lorries and attempted to leave the
city, only to be stopped by the authorities. Cavalry patrols
trotted round the streets, but the vast mass of the native
population carried on with their work without any show of
excitement.

Rumours came thick and fast, Dessie was in flames;
Abyssinian troops had counter-attacked during the night
and massacred thousands of Italians. These and a whole
host of other stories were of course all found later to be
completely inaccurate.

During the first few weeks of the war the news from
Addis was worth its weight in gold and that, in fact, is what
it cost the newspaper offices and news agencies. Every
word wirelessed by the journalists from Addis during the
first fortnight of hostilities cost 2s. 6d. That was the urgent
rate charge. As everybody was cabling "urgents" nobody
got any advantage except the cable company and the
Abyssinian Government, which shared the profits. During
one week-end alone the wireless station handled thirty

thousand words. The sensible thing would have been for the journalists to come to an agreement only to send "copy" at normal rates, but with 100 journalists representing a dozen different nationalities, all competing and suspicious of each other, such an agreement was out of the question. Nobody would trust anybody else.

There was great elation in Addis when news was received that an Italian aeroplane had been shot down in the Aussa country. The pilot of the aeroplane spotted a large caravan of camels wending its way through the desert and diving low, opened a machine gun on the animals. The ancient camel driver looked critically at the plane and commented to his companion: "Surely that is the strange bird that Haile Selassie told us to shoot at." At this the camel driver raised his rifle, took a pot shot, and by some miracle brought the plane down. Both pilot and observer were killed instantaneously. The camel driver and his companions then cut off the wings of the aeroplane "so it could not fly away again."

Then a flutter was caused in diplomatic circles in Addis by the Count Vinci episode. Count Vinci was the Italian Minister to the court of Haile Selassie. For months he had been the brain of an elaborate spy system and organization of agents which worked pro-Italian propaganda throughout the country. In the days immediately before the war he was the source of considerable embarrassment to the Ethiopian Government. The Italians were trying hard to find an incident which would justify their aggressive intentions and Count Vinci deliberately invited trouble. He insisted on walking unattended in the most undesirable and lonely parts of the town. Every afternoon he sat alone in a vast empty house, which had formerly been the Fascist club, on the pretext of being available to the journalists. From my knowledge of Vinci I am convinced that he

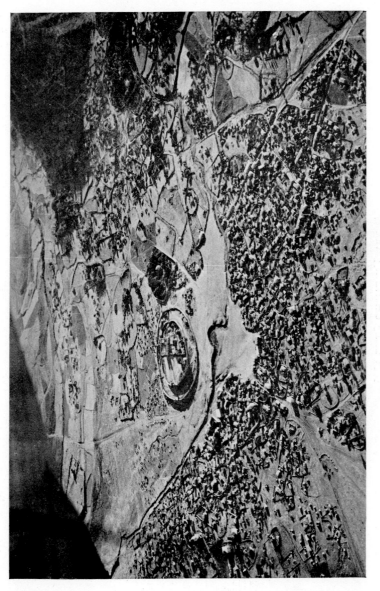

ADOWA, UNCHANGED SINCE 1896

deliberately set himself up as a target in the hope of giving Mussolini an excuse for war.

When at the outbreak of hostilities Vinci was given his passport he refused to leave. His reason was that the Italian consular agent from Magalo was still not safely out of the country. Like the captain of a sinking ship Count Vinci maintained that he should be the last to leave. He locked himself in his Legation and it took hours of skilful diplomacy by the Ethiopian Government to induce him finally to become their guest in a neighbouring country house. Here he remained a virtual prisoner for a fortnight until his consular agent reached the Addis to Djibouti railway.

I was travelling up the railway from Harar to Addis when our train stopped at Afdem station. A down train had also stopped at the station. Suddenly I noticed the drawn blinds of a wagon-lit raised a few inches and a hand waving to me from under it. Behind the hand was the face of Count Vinci smiling in recognition. I went over to try to speak to him but was promptly stopped by an Abyssinian guard with fixed bayonets. So the Italian Minister left Abyssinia.

And all the while the journalists were clamouring in vain to be allowed to go to the front.

While we were still waiting impatiently the big armies which had been recruited in the provinces of Kambata, Jimma, and Kafa in South-west Abyssinia—districts unlikely to be affected by the war—arrived in Addis on their way to the Northern front. Fierce warriors, many of whom had never seen a motor car or a white man before, swarmed into the capital, singing their war songs and brandishing swords and spears. I tried to pass a contingent of them in my car in the town one day but I received such menacing looks that I waited until they were well out of the way

before going on. One journalist was indiscreet enough
to try to pass through the ranks of a marching column of
these warriors. He was dragged from his car and found
himself with several spears at his throat. He was saved
by an Abyssinian policeman.

Barefooted, wild and bearded, many of them had dyed
their normally white robes a pinkish brown in muddy
streams on the march up as a camouflage against Italian
marksmen. At one time there were over forty thousand
of them in the city. They besieged the Gebbi (palace)—
shouting for the Emperor, clamouring for guns and ammunition, and boasting their bravery. In return the Emperor
entertained contingent after contingent of them to feasts
of raw meat. The modern Abyssinian is rather ashamed of
these orgies, which are relics of the days when Abyssinia
was at war with the Dervishes and unable to light fires for
fear of revealing their positions to the enemy. These feasts
were rather too much for the Emperor, who has European
tastes in food, but had to participate out of politeness.
Weekly doses of "Kosso," the Abyssinian equivalent of
Beecham's Pills, helped the Emperor to survive these ordeals.

The armies camped in the plains surrounding the capital
and a visit one night to the camp of Dedjazmatch Mashasha,
Governor of Kambata, gave me a vivid picture of an
Abyssinian night's entertainment. The plain was flooded
with moonlight. Woods of blue gum trees stood like a
regiment of silver sentinels, and the mountains which form
a natural battlement round Addis were sharply silhouetted
in support of a vast inverted bowl of stars.

In the heart of the plain was a city of tents, with hundreds
of camp fires. Ghostlike figures flittered about the camp.
Somebody was singing an age-old battle-song. Dogs barked
and a warrior who had had more liquor than was good for
him let off a gun.

UNDER FIRE WITH THE EMPEROR

From the pavilion of Fitaorari Zalaka came sounds of revelry. The Fitaorari and his wife were entertaining their sub-chiefs. A boy stood in the pavilion holding a blazing torch. The Fitaorari and his good lady sat on a carpet covered divan with their guests squatting round on the floor in a circle. A bullock had been killed and skinned and every guest had his chunk of red and steaming meat. Mrs. Fitaorari took one end of a succulent piece of flesh in her left hand and placed the other end between her teeth. A deft upward slash of the knife in the right hand and madam was busily chewing—the knife having flashed past her nose a hair's breadth away. Had she carved downwards she would have bespattered her gown with meat juices. The guests followed her example and the meat was washed down with copious draughts of "tej," a potent native drink, similar to mead.

The camp jester—a dwarf—twanged a one-stringed guitar and sang his jests.

His great joke was to sing in a basso profundo and then suddenly switch into a high-pitched treble.

Suddenly a warrior leaped to his feet and dashed out of the tent to make the night outside hideous with blood-curdling war cries. Two boys drew back the flaps of the tent. The warrior returned. For a moment he was framed in the entrance, the central figure of a dramatic tableau, with the triangle of night sky of the tent entrance at his back. With blazing eyes and uplifted spear he charged the Fitaorari. The spear-point stopped within an inch of the Fitaorari's throat. The chief did not so much as flinch. Leaping back a pace or two the warrior stabbed and jabbed with his spear, miming how he would fight for the Fitaorari, and all the time boasting his prowess in war.

Like a chorus the remainder of the guests leaped to their feet, shouting and dancing. Guest after guest left the tent, returned and repeated the performance. Young men and grey-bearded warriors who had fought at Adowa joined in the ceremony. Many of the guests completed their performance by kissing the feet of the Fitaorari. One young brave became so dangerous with his long curved sword that he had to be forcibly removed. Another fired off his rifle and the bullet made a neat hole in the canvas of the tent.

At last the Fitaorari stood up and raised his right hand. The "party" was over. The guests drained their gourds of tej and departed into the night. Lights in the tents flickered out and silence fell on the moonlit plain.

The next day the Fitaorari and his men marched into the mountains to brave the artillery, machine guns, tanks, aeroplanes, and poison gas of the Italians with their swords, spears, and antiquated rifles.

At last I was given permission to go to Dessie which was to become the Ethiopian General Headquarters in the north. I hired a lorry, bought food for a month, and loaded up with many cases of petrol at the Central African price of five shillings a gallon. With about half a ton of kit and an Abyssinian "caravan" staff consisting of chauffeur, chauffeur's boy, cook and cook's boy, a personal servant and an interpreter I jolted off in the lorry along the Great North Road which runs for two hundred miles from Addis to Dessie.

The road at its best is a mere flattened mud track which switchbacks like a giant racer up and down the mountains, frequently running on the top of precipices. At one moment the road is eleven thousand feet above sea level and within half an hour by car it has plunged down a matter of six thousand feet into baking hot valleys. It is a remarkable engineering feat considering that most of it has been carved out of sheer mountain-side by native workmen, using curved sticks with a small iron point as their principal tool.

UNDER FIRE WITH THE EMPEROR

Along this road over a quarter of a million men of the armies of Ethiopia marched to meet the Italians. As I jogged along in my lorry I ran into one army on the move. There were no trim battalions marching four abreast, no wheeled transport of any kind, just a straggling procession of men and mules spread over a distance of five or six miles.

There were women carrying gourds of drink, small boys struggling along with tent poles, mules, horses and donkeys loaded with ammunition boxes, tents, sacks and hay. We passed a little group carrying the war drums pannier-wise on mules. We raised our hats to the chiefs who invariably rode mule-back in the shade of an umbrella. Some kept to the road but many took the shorter rocky caravan trails which cut straight over the mountain. The only modern touch along the roadside was the telephone booth, a relic of the Emperor Menelik who forty years ago realised the importance of speedy communication in controlling his Empire.

The first day's journey ran across a series of plains of rich black soil suitable for cotton growing but barren of everything except grass. I camped for the night in the shelter of a small hill for protection from the cold night wind and the Abyssinian kitchen department showed us it could serve a passable meal of four courses. The following day I was stopped at Debra Birham, a military post and telephone station where I learned that there had been trouble on the road between the Imperial Guard and the irregular troops. A quarrel had broken out between some of the irregulars who were jealous of the smart uniforms and superior equipment of the Imperial Guard. Why, demanded the irregulars, should they have to provide their own guns, rifles and food when the Guard were given the best of everything for nothing? Some fighting took place and a number of men on either side were wounded.

ABYSSINIAN STOP PRESS

After Debra Birham the road climbs rapidly into the mountains and as far as the eye can reach are mountain peaks, escarpments, gullies and ravines. An American who was travelling with me said: "Here you have the Grand Canyon of the Colorado, the Rocky Mountains and the Alleghany Mountains all rolled into one." From this point onwards the road runs for the most part along the top of the great mountain wall which separates the central Abyssinian plateau from the Danakil Plain.

At one spot we came suddenly upon a V-shaped gap in the gigantic mountain battlements through which we could see the whole plain stretching away in a haze of blue and gold to Assab, over three hundred miles away on the Red Sea. A little farther on—about 120 miles north-east of Addis Ababa—we reached our highest point, where the road runs nearly twelve thousand feet above sea level. Then it starts to fall down an almost sheer wall of mountain.

Again the view was magnificent. The lowering sun fell in shafts over the top of the mountains like a series of natural spot-lights, giving the foothills two thousand feet below the appearance of a vividly coloured relief map. All over the side of the mountain and on the very edge of the ledge of road down which my lorry crept grew great clusters of blazing red-hot pokers contrasting with delicate flowering rock plants. We had to get the lorry round a series of acute hairpin bends and at each bend the boys had to climb out and wedge stones under the front wheels to prevent us from skidding over the side of the precipices.

After the nerve strain of this descent we camped early that evening at the foot of the mountain. The tents were only just up when two soldiers arrived to ask who we were. We told them, and presently they returned bearing as gifts a live kid, a quantity of cooked meat, native bread and tej. Their chief was Dedjazmatch Matafferi who had moved from his headquarters at the town of Ankober to await beside the road the coming of the Emperor on his way to Dessie. The Dedjazmatch, we were told, would visit us next morning.

The following morning we had breakfasted, struck tents, packed the lorry and were all ready to move on by 8.30. There was no sign of the Dedjazmatch. Anxious to push on we decided to call on the Dedjazmatch and walked to his village, about half a dozen native huts surrounded by a palisade of thorn bushes.

The Dedjazmatch received us in one of the huts sitting on a couch covered with a carpet. Behind him hung his revolver, ammunition belt and a pair of binoculars. The Abyssinian of rank has dignity and good manners and our conversation, carried on through my interpreter, followed the most formal lines. The Dedjazmatch particularly wanted to know about the health of the Emperor and the date he would pass through his territory.

"When soldiers go to war in your country," he asked "are they given tea and coffee, meat and flour?"

When I told him that they were he pondered for a few moments and then commented rather solemnly: "When we go to war we have to provide everything for ourselves. I sometimes think we give our Government too much."

After having just had an excellent breakfast I was horrified to find that a banquet was being prepared in my honour. The Dedjazmatch went off to supervise the arrangements, and a few minutes later I was shown into another hut. Here the Dedjazmatch motioned me to be seated on a low stool beside an equally low basket-work table. There were no knives or forks and no plates. On the table before me was a sheet of *ingera* (native bread). In colour and texture it looks very similar to tripe—thin and flabby, smooth one side and honeycombed the other.

A serving maid ladled me a generous helping of *wop* (stewed mincemeat), which is pink with red pepper and hotter than the hottest curry. The Dedjazmatch tore off a piece of his bread, used it to mop up a quantity of the meat and placed it in my mouth with his own fingers. As I ate my throat blazed with fire and beads of perspiration came out on my forehead. But there was no escape. The Dedjazmatch continued to roll me ball after ball of ingera and wop. This was swilled down with horn beakers full of tej. Any qualms I had about swallowing dysentery germs in native drinks went by the board in my desire to extinguish the fire in my throat. Finally when the demands of Abyssinian etiquette were satisfied I was able to leave but even then the Dedjazmatch insisted on giving me three of his soldiers as guard for the rest of the journey.

By this time the sun was hot and after one English breakfast and one Abyssinian banquet . . . well, one was not feeling too fit. Still even so I should hate to believe it was the Dedjazmatch's tej which caused me to slip off some stepping stones crossing the next ford and land on my hands and knees in the stream!

The previous evening we had shivered on the mountain top and piled on pullovers and overcoats. But as we plunged lower and lower into one of the great valleys which opens through the mountain escarpment into the Danakil plain the sun became fiercely tropical. Here the road ran through plantations of sugar canes, cotton, and mealies. Watchtowers consisting of four posts with a birds' nest platform perched on the top, which I have seen photographed and described in the newspapers as military look-outs, were really supports for small boys who scared the birds off the crops. What looked like rolls of matting hanging from trees were Abyssinian beehives. Monkeys were swinging about in creeper-hung trees; birds of brilliant plumage fluttered up in alarm at our lorry but guineafowl were so tame that they did not trouble to move until our wheels were almost on top of them.

Once the lorry stuck in the bed of a boulder strewn stream. All the kit had to be unloaded and carried ashore and finally the cook's boy had to assume the rôle of diver to remove a rock in the way of the differential.

Intensive cultivation is not common in Abyssinia. The whole countryside is dotted with tiny villages whose inhabitants are too lazy to grow more than their bare necessities, but that night we camped in a valley where every square inch of available space was cultivated. From above it the well defined fields gave the appearance of a patchwork quilt.

On the third day we saw the corrugated iron roofs of Dessie perched on the top of a plateau among the mountain peaks in front of us. As the crow flies the town was only a few miles away, but the road managed to climb and dive in a series of switchbacking spirals for another twenty miles, most of which was along the ledge of a precipice.

Dessie, normally the seat of the Crown Prince, is huddled in a lofty valley, 8,000 feet above sea level. A hundred other mountain peaks crowd round it. It is little more than a village of native huts and boasts only of about a dozen stone buildings. When I arrived the few Greek and Armenian store keepers were busily packing up their wares for flight to Addis. The only other white residents in the town were four American missionaries in charge of the Seventh Day Adventist's Hospital and two French priests.

The one imposing building was the former Italian Consulate which was to become the Emperor's General Headquarters. With its pleasant gardens it made a striking contrast to the ramshackle collection of corrugated iron-roofed buildings on a neighbouring hill top which was the residence of the Crown Prince and his tutor, Dedjazmatch Wadaje.

We set up our camp in the compound of the missionary hospital where I am afraid the missionaries eyed us with some apprehension. The trouble was that the first journalist who arrived in Dessie had breezed into the mission and brightly asked whether Dr. Stedene, the head of the mission, could lend him a bottle of whisky! As the missionaries had been teaching their flock the virtues of pure water, some twenty hard-drinking journalists who suddenly settled in their midst must have been something of an embarrassment.

News that the Emperor was on his way to Dessie set the place in a turmoil of excitement. True to their policy of *"eche nhaga"* ("yes to-morrow") everything had been left to the last minute.

There was no washing bowl for the Emperor. The town was searched in vain for a washing utensil and at last Captain Brophil, the Irish Transport Officer to No. 3 unit of the Ethiopian Red Cross, produced an enamel bowl with the request that it should be returned when the Emperor had no further use for it. A feverish attempt was made to build a new road for the Emperor's car but this had to be abandoned half completed. An hour before the Emperor was due to arrive the whole town, including women and children, was at work filling up pot-holes in the old road with baskets of earth.

Although the Emperor's car was sighted only a few miles away at 4 o'clock that afternoon and a great parade of troops and town folk was drawn up to welcome him, the Emperor waited outside until after dark and then slipped unseen into the town.

The next morning the Emperor was already installed in the former Italian Consulate which for the next three

months was Ethiopia's G.H.Q. With only three private
secretaries who knew any language but their own—sharing
one old typewriter between them—the Emperor administered
the Empire, ran the war and carried on diplomatic negotiations with the League of Nations and the Great Powers
which were either trying to solve his troubles or create new
ones for him.

It was a marvel to me how this frail little man—the
complete physical opposite of the brawny Italian dictator—
could cram so much work into the twenty-four hours.
Every day he was up by 5 a.m. and usually he spent half
an hour in prayer in the little chapel adjoining headquarters.
At 6.30 a.m. he took his breakfast, which included coffee
and a little meat, except on fast days—and there are an
inordinate number of fasts in the Ethiopian calendar—when
he only ate a few mouthfuls of grain and drank a glass of
water.

Immediately after breakfast the mail, brought by runners
who carry letters in cleft sticks, by lorry, or by internal
air mail, which the war had forced upon Ethiopia, was placed
before the Emperor. In addition to letters and reports from
all over the Empire there would be wireless messages from
Europe and dispatches from the Generals in the field.
Sometimes the Emperor was faced with an hour's solid
reading. Another hour would be occupied by his majesty
in replying to this correspondence. The Emperor had
brought the art of dictating to his three secretaries at the
same time to a high pitch of efficiency. He would dictate
half a letter to Secretary No. 1, then switch over to Secretary No. 2 while Secretary No. 1 was transcribing his
notes. And by the time he had finished with Secretary
No. 3 the Emperor would be dictating the second half of the
first letter to Secretary No. 1. Invariably he could take
up the thread of each letter without being prompted. The

remainder of the morning was taken up by audiences with visiting chiefs or officers who had returned from the front.

Instead of taking the afternoon nap advised by his doctor the Emperor would go for a short walk, but by 3 o'clock there was usually another pile of urgent telegrams to be dealt with. As the genuine Commander-in-Chief of his forces the whole strategy of the war rested on his shoulders. A telegram saying that the Italians had advanced, say, near Makale, and the Emperor would call as many as a dozen people who knew that particular country into consultation. When he had assimilated all they had to say about the topography he would draw his own map and issue instructions to his commanders on the spot. In European manner he would drink a cup of tea while he worked and usually his work took him well past dinner time—to the exasperation of the royal cooks.

After dinner the Emperor would frequently take another short walk. Then came the most important task of the day. The Emperor would go into his study to meditate on his problems. No one dared to interrupt him. Usually his light burned there until eleven o'clock but sometimes it was not extinguished until the early hours. But this amazing man was always up again by 5 o'clock the next morning.

One day I made a pilgrimage with the Emperor to Lake Haik. The lake, 20 miles north of Dessie, is sunk in a bowl of mountains and bears a striking resemblance to a Scottish loch. It is seven miles long and about three miles broad. Close to the western shore is a small island on which there is a monastery, which is virtually the Public Records Office of Ethiopia, for the priests guard there most of Ethiopia's State and religious manuscripts. The island is approached by a ferry boat—a bundle of reeds lashed together with rope. When there is more than one passenger the boat is almost entirely under water. The Emperor looked at it critically and decided to receive the priests on the mainland. One of the priests is reputed to be 107 years of age.

Our biggest excitement in Dessie was the Italian airraid when the missionary hospital and our own camp was bombed. It was 8 o'clock and a perfect summer morning when we heard the drone of aero engines. Almost simultaneously a gun on the mountain top above the consulate fired three shots—the air-raid warning. A few seconds later we saw four silver-winged Caproni bombing planes entering the Dessie valley from the north. They were flying at about 5,000 feet and as they approached the town a terrific barrage of machine gun and rifle fire was opened at them. Every man with a gun blazed away although the aeroplanes were well out of range.

The Emperor, despite the pleadings of his staff that he should take cover, ran out into the garden of the consulate and opened fire with an anti-aircraft gun.

The aeroplanes flew in formation over the town, turned and then, splitting formation, criss-crossed backwards and forwards, dropping bombs. Tall columns of white smoke rose from the town, marking the spots where high explosive bombs had fallen. I saw native huts burst into flames and men, women and children rushing for cover.

At the cross roads in the centre of the town there was almost indescribable horror. In the dense smoke from a score of heavy bombs against a background of flame from a dozen or more burning buildings men and mules were stampeding for safety over the bodies of the dead and dying.

And all the while the Emperor went on firing his anti-aircraft gun. Soldiers threw a cloak round his shoulders to conceal his uniform and urged him to come away but he waved them aside. He was joined by his thirteen year old son, the Duke of Harar.

The Crown Prince's palace on the hill was struck by a bomb, and a church went up in flames. While bombs were still falling, Captain M. Brophil of the Ethiopian Red Cross, and his colleague, Mr. Hickey, came down into the centre of the town and started first-aid work. After the raid had been on for a quarter of an hour another six aeroplanes arrived, but they circled the outskirts of the town apparently looking for military camps.

The journalists were too excited by what was to them "a good news story" to remember to don gas masks or even to take cover. They either raced about taking photographs or stood staring at the planes through binoculars. But before the raid was over they too had their baptism of fire. The raid had been on for about fifty minutes when the first four planes to arrive took up formation again and flew northwards down the Dessie valley. As they passed over the hospital they loosed a shower of incendiary bombs. Three of them smashed through the hospital's corrugated iron roof, passing through the very centre of the painted red cross. Another twenty or so fell in the compound among the tents of the journalists. Just twenty paces to my left a bomb set the grass on fire and the same distance to my right a second bomb set the medical store tent on fire. Another bomb fell beside the tent of Mr. Harrison the *Reuter* correspondent. The hospital was on fire but the missionaries were able to extinguish it.

By this time the wounded—most of them civilians—were being brought in. An emergency dressing and sorting station was opened in the shade of the eucalyptus trees while in the hospital Dr. Stedene, assisted by Swedish and German doctors from the various Red Cross units, started operating. From 9 o'clock in the morning till 9 o'clock at night they performed one operation after another. When darkness fell they went on with their work by the light of motor car head-lamps, shining through the window of the operating theatre. I saw one woman who had had both her legs and both breasts blown away, and she lived until the next day.

There were the beginnings of an ugly anti-white demonstration immediately after the raid when photographers and cinema-men started taking pictures of the wreckage. M. Georges Goyon, the correspondent of the French Havas Agency, who was riding in a lorry through the town, was shot at by an Abyssinian and wounded in the leg, the same bullet, passing through the trouser leg of Captain A. Varges, an American cinema man. I took some photographs of some burning huts but the attitude of the natives was so hostile that I retreated into the hospital compound. To my mind this demonstration was, if unwarranted, at least understandable. I wondered what would have happened to black men, say in the Tottenham Court Road if London had just been bombed by negro airmen.

Before the bombs had finished falling the newspaper men were typing descriptions of the raid and the Emperor, realizing that it was probably the first time in history that the Press had ever seen a Red Cross hospital bombed, gave orders that all dispatches from Dessie were to be given priority.

That night, in anticipation of another raid the next day, the Emperor gave orders for the evacuation of the town and strict instructions that no more bullets were to be wasted in shooting at aeroplanes which were obviously out of range. Sure enough the Italian bombing planes arrived at the same time the following morning and it spoke well of the Emperor's authority and of the Abyssinian's capacity for learning from his errors that the entire town was empty and that not a single shot was fired.

ABYSSINIAN STOP PRESS

After flying over the town apparently to photograph the damage of the previous day the aeroplanes circled the surrounding country, bombing military camps and the aerodrome. I watched them from the hospital compound. On the hillside some two miles away were a cluster of several dozen tents. Suddenly two aeroplanes dived at them and released a rain of incendiary bombs. A dense cloud of smoke arose and when it had cleared a few minutes later not a tent was to be seen.

The raids only made one man happy—the bank manager. He, an Abyssinian educated in London, was delighted that his bank had been bombed because it would enable him to build a "palatial" new one for a matter of thirty thalers (about £2 10s.)!

The next day the Emperor attended a service ordered by the missionaries in thanksgiving for their escape during the air-raids. The service was held in the missionaries' garden. Afternoon sunshine streamed through the blue-green eucalyptus trees and fell on the little group of Europeans and Abyssinians who joined in prayer. Birds sang and tame deer ambled through the open air church. A dignified figure in his field marshal's uniform, the Emperor followed the service, which was translated from English into Amharic, with close attention.

Afterwards the Emperor visited the hospital to see the air-raid wounded. Cameramen were invited into the operating theatre to take photographs of the Emperor watching an operation. The pictures duly appeared in the world's newspapers under such captions as "Emperor watching an operation on a victim of the Dessie air-raids."

Actually the operation was on a man whose hand had been cut off by a local chief as punishment for stealing a few handfuls of hay. But it is only fair to say that neither the Emperor nor the photographers knew this at the time.

TINY ABYSSINIAN HUTS—POOR TARGETS FOR ITALIAN BOMBS

Such are the barbarities which the Emperor, as a civilised and cultured man, was working to stamp out when his social reforms were brought to a standstill by the Italian aggression.

A day or so later all the Europeans in Dessie were invited to dine with the Emperor in the Palace on the hill. It was a moonlit night and as we climbed the precipitous path to the Palace the silvery peaks of the surrounding mountains stood out in shining contrast to the blackness of the shadowed valleys. In the moonlight the Palace, which by daylight looks like a collection of dilapidated cowsheds, took on the appearance of a mediæval castle. Guides holding flaming torches lighted our footsteps, and sentries with long spears gave silent salutes. But inside the mediæval fantasy was lost in shabby modern furniture, petrol vapour lamps, ghastly patterned wall papers and cheap Japanese prints.

It must have been the worst dressed royal dinner party in history. For want of better clothes we turned up in a strange medley of khaki, sports jackets, and pullovers. My "best" consisted of riding breeches and a leather golf jacket and from a sartorial point of view the journalist who mustered a creased lounge suit took first prize. So we shook hands, sipped cocktails and presently broke bread with the ever dignified ruler of some twelve million people, immaculate as ever in his service uniform.

Life at Dessie soon became monotonous. For want of something to do we organised mountaineering expeditions and climbed to peaks where eagles soared round our heads and where frightened baboons loosed showers of stones at us as they scurried away. We gave as elaborate dinner parties as we could concoct from our limited stock of tinned fare and local food stuff. Our supplies of drink, tobacco and reading materials ran short. Letters and newspapers which were weeks old only reached us after long intervals.

The scarcity of news from the outside world was perhaps our greatest loss and there was always a stampede in the camp when a communique of European news or a despatch from the front was pinned on our tree-trunk notice-board. For a brief fortnight we had a wireless set to relieve our boredom. We were thrilled to hear "London" and to listen to Italian reporters in Asmara dictating their articles from the wireless telephone in Eritrea to their offices in Rome. But something went wrong with the set and after the Emperor's wireless "expert" had put an eight volt instead of a four volt battery on to it, in his attempts at repair, the set never spoke again.

We bought pack and riding mules to take us to the front and when we asked when we should be allowed to go and see the fighting we were invariably told "in a few days now." But those few days came and went many times and still we remained in Dessie. Nerves became strained with the lack of activity. One journalist hit another in the jaw and subsequently was fined heavily in the American Consular Court in Addis Ababa; and there was a stand-up fight between a German and a Greek doctor over a small matter relating to their mess accounts.

There was a certain amount of humorous relief in trying to evade the censorship. It was not difficult to conceal news of vital importance in the middle of an otherwise innocuous message. Or even to leave a space at the top of the paper so as to type in censorable matter after the message had been signed. One journalist got transmitted a message referring to the Emperor as "Ethiopia's big shot No. 1." After laboriously wading through an article of mine a Belgian officer with a poor knowledge of English, who was acting as censor confessed: "You know I cannot read this stuff, but I suppose it's all right." On another

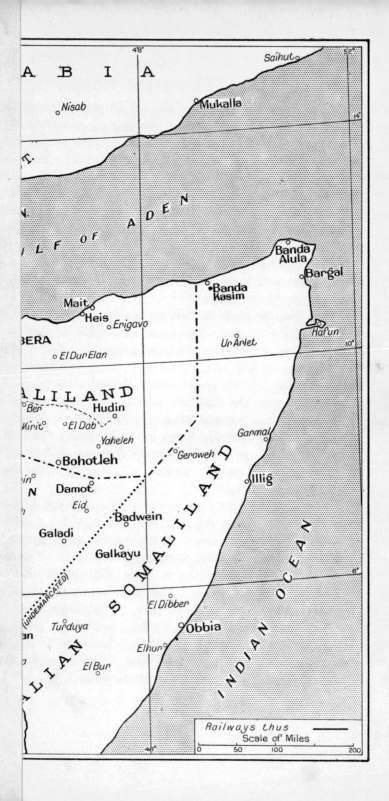

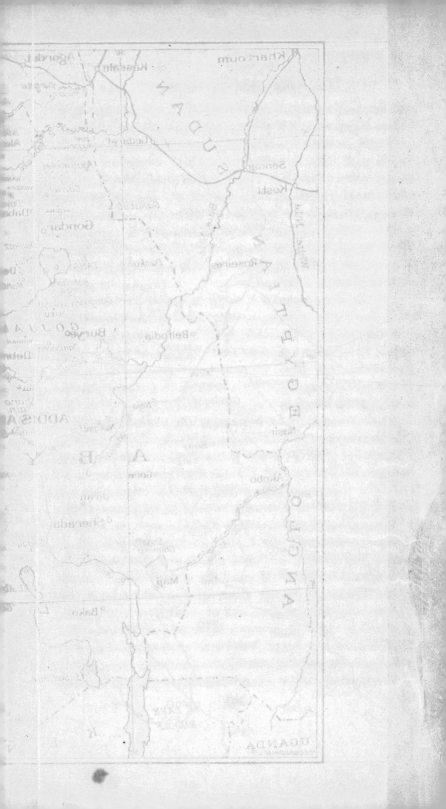

occasion an Abyssinian censor whose English was but little better called me back after passing a message which had started with some important military information but had ended with some harmless news about the effect of the rains on the Italian roads. I thought that I had been caught out after all but the censor's enquiry was merely, "By the way, what is the meaning of the word 'mud?'"

From time to time Italian reconnaissance aeroplanes flew over us, and although no more bombs were dropped, I never got to like those few seconds when the machines seemed directly overhead.

For Christmas a party of us spent several pleasant days at Lake Haik, riding, shooting, swimming, sun-bathing and boating in a collapsible canoe lent us by the missionaries. One bright moment was when our native cook served the cherished Christmas pudding—with mashed potatoes. Apparently he believed this to be some obscure European meat dish.

When it became clear that newspaper interest in the war was waning journalist after journalist received a wireless message, on blue Ethiopian telegraph forms, telling them to come back to Europe. Finally my recall came.

I went to say good-bye to the Emperor. Although this time I was received in a small, barely furnished room, where the only decoration was a large photograph of the Empress and a big scale map of Ethiopia, the interview was just as formal and dignified as when I had seen the Emperor in his expensively furnished palace in Addis.

The Emperor told me that while he was anxious for peace to relieve the sufferings of a poorly-armed people, menaced by the shells, bombs and poison gases of a powerful aggressor, he would accept no peace terms which were outside the spirit and Covenant of the League of Nations.

He thanked me for expressing Ethiopia's case through

my paper and presented me with an autographed photograph of himself firing an anti-aircraft gun, a rhinoceros shield embossed with gilt and silver, and two spears.

The next morning I struck camp, piled my kit and servants into the lorry and set off for Addis. I had wirelessed London that I should be back in the capital in three days—the time it had taken me to do the journey in the opposite direction. I had not foreseen the effect of rain on an Abyssinian road or the perilous inefficiency of a new and untried Abyssinian chauffeur whom I had just acquired.

We set out from Dessie on a dry road and bowled along at a merry pace on the ledge of a precipice until . . . until the Abyssinian driver took a corner too widely. The road in front of the bonnet disappeared into space as the lorry aimed at a tangent for the edge of the precipice. The offside wheels were on the very brink of the drop; the projecting side of the lorry hung over space, and panic-stricken, the driver made an attempt to climb out of the cab, thought better of it, and somehow stopped the lorry. That was the last time I let an Abyssinian touch the driving wheel. His place was taken by a German colleague who proved himself at least a careful driver.

A few miles further on we ran into our first mud! A great spinning of wheels and the lorry sank axle-deep into the mire. We dug the mud away behind the wheels, made a foundation of stones on a level with the treads and jerked the lorry backwards. Then we filled in the holes dug by the spinning wheels with stones, made a carpet of brushwood ahead and with everybody pushing and shoving we were able to move forward on to firm ground.

During the next nine days—so much for my three days' return journey—we repeated this performance at least a hundred times. Sometimes the effort had to be repeated as many as five times to get the lorry up a slope of fifty yards. And every time the same shout went up:

"Dingi! dingi!"　("Stones! stones! !")

"Tinish dingi!"　("Tiny stones!")

"Tollo! tollo! !"　("Quickly! quickly! !")

I learned more Amharic during those muddy ten days than during the whole of the preceding six months I had spent in Abyssinia. To move at all with the lorry it was necessary not only to shout instructions in the language but to keep on shouting them. For the Abyssinian individually hates work, and the idea of working in a team is completely outside his sphere of comprehension.

Consequently every time we stuck in the mud the "boys" remained seated comfortably in the lorry. Every time I had to order them out and start them working.

"Tollo tollo! !"

"Dingi dingi! !"

The interpreter did not expect to do manual work and the cook argued with Abyssinian logic that the task of pushing a one-ton truck did not come under the category of cooking. While I would be getting these two into action the remainder of the staff would take the opportunity for a rest. Soon my voice was hoarse with urging them on. Although this lethargy on the part of the Abyssinian is irritating to the European in a hurry, there is a certain amount of widom in it in a country like Abyssinia. The Abyssinian knows from experience that it is very little use attempting to fight rain and mud. You might just as well camp by the road side until it has stopped raining and the road has dried sufficiently for you to drive in comfort.

Our first big spot of bother came at the Four Bridges— four rickety structures of wood and stones over four small streams. We charged across the first bridge only to sink into the morass into which the recent rain had converted

Dutch ambulances, and five supply lorries. Here we started a two-day battle with the mud, the convoy advancing by a series of jerks a matter of eight miles at a time. The procedure was always the same, the leading British truck having the best tyre treads, carved a track through the mud, a hundred natives pushing and hauling on ropes. Then, by the same process of pulling and shoving, lorry after lorry was dragged forward until the convoy was all together again. And then the effort would be repeated again and again until the light failed.

For two days everybody helped everybody else. We all worked with pick and shovel, we all tugged at the tow ropes and pushed at the back of the lorries, while old Waldi Basha—the local chief—cracked his whip to urge his tribesmen to greater efforts at pulling and shoving.

On the ninth day we climbed Shola Mada, the 11,500-foot mountain which is Ethiopia's last line of defence before Addis Ababa. Fortunately, the tortuous hairpin bends and steep gradients of the mountain road were comparatively dry, but even so it was a matter of leaping quickly out of the lorry at each acute bend to wedge stones under the wheels so that we should not skid backwards over the precipices. We stopped at one spot where the road descends at 1 in 4 and then turns at right angles along a narrow shelf on the top of a precipice. Two thousand feet below lay the wreckage of a lorry. A few days earlier it was descending the slope when the brakes failed and the lorry hurtled over the edge of a precipice with the Greek driver still clinging to the steering wheel.

The following day we arrived in Addis Ababa, to find telegrams awaiting us to know why we had wasted so much time on the road!

THE "BUSU TSHIKI-TSHIK"
(THE GREAT WAR)

BY LADISLAS FARAGO

War-Correspondent to the New York Times and Sunday Chronicle, the only journalist with the Abyssinian Army in the North.

150 "ante-war correspondents"—they had to wait for weeks and months—were given the same information as I in the travel bureaux, so there travelled in the white carriages of the Abyssinian railway—which are now better known than they were eight months ago and which had previously been occupied exclusively by adventurers, big-game hunters and determined merchants—journalists and always more journalists.

Although they did not find a war going on when they arrived, they had to wage a private war of their own. They had to fight for news. Abyssinia offered no organisation to help the crowds of journalists, and apart from that, the months of July, August, and September, even in the atmosphere of threatening war, are a dead season in Abyssinia. Apart from the terrible tropical rain which is so typical of the country nothing whatever happens during this time, and the natives have always been prisoners of the storm. That year the journalists were no exception, and they sat about in the overcrowded hotels, living as many as five in a room, waiting. It takes three days and two nights to travel from Jibuti to Addis Ababa. This antediluvian tempo nearly broke the spirit of these bustling journalists, but after their first week in Addis Ababa they were already feeling that the train had conveyed them too quickly to the capital. For this reason I decided to travel by caravan on my second visit, slow though it is.

Our plan was to travel by Khartoum, Gedaref, and crossing the Abyssinian frontier at Gallabat, to go on to Gondar to strike the most direct route to the theatre of war. The railway does not terminate at Khartoum and one can travel on as far as Gedaref, but the journey from there is not exactly a so-called pleasure trip. The district through which we had to pass on our way to Abyssinia is one of the "closed districts" which may only be visited with special permit. We waited for the permit, and in the meantime we fitted out our caravan. I had a little experience of short caravan journeys, but the longer the trip the longer the list of requirements. If one forgets a needle, a corkscrew or any such trifle, the whole trip can be spoilt. After Khartoum civilisation is gradually left behind. We felt this when we took our leave of the restaurant car at Haya, and when the railway line finished at Gedaref, one still found some traces of European civilisation, but electric light and refrigerators became scarcer and scarcer and the last thing to disappear was whisky which always can be found in the most out-lying villages as long as there is an English commissioner.

We had, as a matter of fact, no difficulties. The officials of the Sudan Government did all they could for us, not only in Khartoum, but also en route. For example in the comfortless desert station of Aroma, an elegant Englishman called out our names and asked whether we wanted to see the town of Kassala where we had to wait for four hours. When we said yes, he immediately sent a telegram to Kassala and the governor's car was awaiting us at the station. Later we were given refreshments at his house. We hardly ever arrived anywhere without an English official appearing who had been informed of our presence by telegraph from the train and he brought us information and refreshments. In Gedaref itself the District Commissioner's car was waiting for us and we were driven to an excellent resthouse, and our brand new tent felt quite offended at being left in its bag. Mr. Morrison, the twenty-nine year old Commissioner, was seeing to the camel drivers who were going to take us the following morning to Gallabat. Only now do I understand the meaning of the Biblical expression of the camel and the needle. Instead of a camel it ought to be a camel driver, for with a camel everything runner to Gondar to get permission from Ras Kassa's son, Dedjaz Wolde Wossen, to order escorts and mules as I could not get any in Gallabat. The messenger searched for Dedjaz Wolde Wossen for days in vain, and eventually returned empty handed.

We had no other course than to break regulations and cross the frontier, illegally, into the country that did not want us. We hired camels which are uncommon in Abyssinia and aroused great commotion on that account. We paid the Shum our dues—he looks after all business in small frontier villages—and set out for Abyssinia. The trip was very hard, tiring, uncomfortable and terribly expensive for every village we passed we had to pay more "dues."

Gallabat, the tiny village in British Sudan, was for us the last outpost of civilisation. It had a telegraph office and also the means of despatching letters, admittedly only twice a month, for during the rainy season the mail is carried by camels. At this point I had to organise a regular news service if I wanted my despatches and the photographs of my companion, Rudolph Crohn, to reach Europe. Apart from Addis Ababa and a few towns in the east, there are no post offices or telegraph stations in all Abyssinia.

. . . . .

My arrival in the tiny post office caused considerable excitement. The postmaster to whom I presented my "collect press pass" which entitled me to send telegrams free of charge, himself an Abyssinian, disclosed to me that he had wide experience in receiving and transmitting telegrams as he was used to sending on an average as many as sixty words a month. On the same evening I appeared with my first dispatch numbering 1,700 words. The poor

MOBILISATION IN HARAR

fellow turned pale with horror. In his mind he figured out that this would mean sitting all night at the "Morse" —so he preferred a sudden attack of malaria.

"It is impossible, Mr. Farago," he said terrified, "I am ill, I must go to bed at once."

Later on, when he saw that there was no getting rid of me, he applied to Khartoum for an assistant. The assistant came by camel and when he arrived he already had malaria.

In Gallabat I employed two reliable runners who accompanied me on the journey and ran back from time to time to Gallabat with my post. From there letters were taken by the post office to Gedaref. Gedaref is connected with Khartoum by a twice-weekly train service and the Imperial Airways take letters and pictures from there to London.

My telegrams were sent to Gallabat and from there they were wirelessed to Gedaref. Gedaref wirelessed them on to Khartoum, Khartoum telegraphed them to Cairo and from there they were sent to London. The runners took four days to get from North Abyssinia to Gallabat and another four from Gallabat to Gedaref. Once Gedaref has been reached everything goes much quicker and if the runner reaches that town on Friday evening, London receives them on the following Saturday forenoon. It sometimes happened that the runners were late and then my telegrams overlapped.

Such was the method of my news service and I am convinced that I had to pay the highest rate for letters of all time. An Abyssinian runner who took my post to Gallabat got 28s., and the messenger from Gallabat to Gedaref 20s. I worked it out that a letter on the average, cost 12s.

When the runners returned they brought my post which in the meantime had arrived in Gedaref or Gallabat, and what was still more important, telegraphed news from the English Reuter agency, which one can subscribe to for one pound a month. These telegrams consisted of extracts from the news of the day and they kept me continually informed about what was going on in the world. So it was, that although I was in a sea of ignorance in Abyssinia, I myself knew about everything that was happening—four to six days later—whether it was the birth of the Duke of Kent's son or economic sanctions of the League of Nations against Italy.

The getting of news was far more difficult than its transmission. My pitch was as big as England, Scotland and Wales and our movements by camel were incredibly slow, indeed we felt lucky if we covered thirty-five kilometres per day, but here again my runners did good service. I always had several messengers under way and they could cover as much as sixty to eighty kilometres a day. They brought me exact information as to the lie of the land, so that I could plan out my route beforehand.

The great difficulty about finding news was that the Abyssinians have a colourful imagination and told me everything, and not only what I wanted to know, and I had to ask hundreds of questions before I heard the facts that I needed.

Rudolph Crohn's work was doubly hard, for he had to develop his photographs as well as take them.

At first photographing was easy enough, but afterwards the Abyssinians made all kinds of difficulties and we had to fight for every picture. Crohn had to take risks, too, for he often went on far ahead of us, or visited villages whose inhabitants lived in fear of air attacks, and wherever he went he had to have his pockets full of small change before he could be successful. He had to distribute tips widely, and the Abyssinian soldiers were delighted to have found a second means of livelihood. Crohn can say indeed that, in this part of the front at least, he financed the war.

What was more difficult even was night photography. Once, when the news arrived that the Abyssinians had laid low 2,500 Italians near Adowa, the village where we were staying arranged great festivities, a so-called fantasia by night. Crohn tried to take some flashlight photographs, but as soon as he made the first flare, the Abyssinians grew excited, thinking that the Italians had arrived or that bombs were being dropped, and Crohn had to give up taking photographs.

When dusk fell and we fled before the attack of the malaria carrying mosquitoes under our mosquito nets, and soon fell asleep after the day's exertions, his second job began and he had to do his developing. He set up an improvised laboratory under a mosquito net in the bush, under the open sky. Sometimes the moonshine disturbed him. As the average day temperature was between 120 and 140 degrees Fahrenheit and the nights were only cooler if a north wind blew, and as the highest temperature that the sensitive films could bear was eighty-one degrees Fahrenheit, his work could not usually begin before midnight.

Crohn was also hindered by the natural problems of the country, especially the water problem, as he required large supplies of water for his developing and we came across wells at infrequent intervals on our journeys. Our small supply of pure drinking water which we carried with us in tanks, we were never keen to hand over, so he had to employ Abyssinians who fetched water from distant wells. He had often to wait for days before he got his supply, and when it eventually arrived it was sometimes heated by the fierce sunrays to a temperature of 100-110 degrees Fahrenheit, and he had to cool it before use. He had different methods of expediting this process, but nevertheless this Abyssinian journey was a wearying and unforgettable experience for this young fellow of twenty-two. He will always remember how at night he developed his films under the glorious star-lit sky of Abyssinia accompanied by the roar of lions and not infrequently by visits from hyenas.

The third member of our party was a Dutchman. He was our leader, interpreter and adviser. He had a wealth of experiences and of Christian names. He was called in full Joseph Ernst Ludwig Nauss, and had first come to Abyssinia exactly ten years before. He had a flair for tourism and had travelled all over the country, which he knew better than any, in a Ford lorry which he had converted into a charabanc. We were fortunate to meet him in Khartoum and to have him—the eternal adventurer —offer to come with us.

I must confess that without Joseph Ernst Ludwig, we should have achieved considerably less, for he could speak Amharic, as well as the special language which one must use if one wants to get anything out of the shums. His great gift for things mechanical turned much useless and rusted Abyssinian war material to good use; he bullied camels and camel drivers, understood how to make fire with two sticks, as he once had to do when our matches ran out, besides which he had a corn which was a most reliable barometer.

During the eight weeks of our work together, he became a complete journalist, but he always longed to go back to the river Birbir where he had washed for gold two years before, and had found nothing. I know that he loved the river and not the gold which he searched for in vain.

* * * * *

THE "BUSU TSHIKI-TSHIK"

On my arrival in Abyssinia, the Abyssinian people did not realise that the "busu tshiki-tshik" was being pushed forward in a long line from North to South, and although the inhabitants of this little village where I then was were debating all day long about the prospects of the war and its possible effects, they had no idea that it had already started. I sat among them, listening but saying nothing, for it would have been dangerous for me to tell them of the attack on Adowa. The village of Mortalkhor where I was, was an example of typical Abyssinian conditions. For the moment, it was practically empty. Men and women, old and young, had left, taking their animals with them, they had not gone to the war, as many would like to think, but had left for a far more peaceful reason. They all escaped when the first rains came and went up to the plateaux at the top of the blue mountains nearby to work for a short time tilling the soil. Every Abyssinian has deeply rooted in his heart the desire to till the soil. But Nature, who has made this great country an almost impregnable fortress of rock, does not allow much bounty in this respect, and grants the Abyssinians only three months to fulfil their greatest wish, and for twelve weeks the plateaux of some eight to fourteen thousand feet become luxuriant estates, where cotton, coffee, and maize grow in large quantities, where the pastures provide the zebus with rich grazing, and where the Abyssinians, from August to October, work as peasants. Half of the country's population were, at the time when the war started, in the mountains, thinking only of farming and not of the war.

The "commandant" of this small village, Balambaras Tagegne, alone had stayed behind. When I visited him he was lying flat out on his bed, trying with every imaginable native medicine to drive out the Devil from his body.

He was suffering from malaria and all manner of illnesses which did not allow him a moment's ease, night or day. It is these illnesses that make old haggard men out of the fine-looking Abyssinians. This old man had one foot in the grave, and although I knew that I could at least cure his malaria with quinine, I hesitated to give it to him, for if he died after I had treated him, the natives would think that I had poisoned him. For this reason I had to look on while he tried to effect a cure with lemon juice. Poor devil!

I only mention Balambaras Tagegne because he seemed to me to be typical. He was not the only Abyssinian chief who lies apathetically in his hut, deadly ill and without interest. The hut of this shum, as the provincial chiefs are called, was quite as wretched as those of the natives and my own, and quite as primitive and dirty. The old man himself slept on an open native bed, his best clothes serving him for a pillow. Alongside stood a European bed carefully draped with a new mosquito-net, but Balambaras Tagegne never spent his night on it, for it was reserved for his goats and hens, which count for more than men in this country.

Behind the bed stood four ancient Mannlicher rifles. Heaven knows how they got to Mortalkhor! On closer examination they seemed to be in working order, but I could not find any kind of munition or bullets. Then Balambaras Tagegne explained in a weak voice that he had none. And the soldiers neither. No, and not even any arms for the few men who had stayed behind, and they would have to put up what fight they could with spears and their curved sabres, if the Italians appeared to-morrow, or the day after in their village. This village lay in the path of the war, and yet it was completely unarmed, just as the hundreds and thousands of similar Abyssinian villages, which awaited developments, without getting news or realising how near they were to danger. But they are fatalistic. The men discussed the position in loud voices in front of the chief's hut. Their hearts beat faster and their blood seemed to course more swiftly through their veins, and when one talked with them, they appeared heroic and determined, and if I had not already known that in their hearts doubts were arising, I might easily have imagined their strength to be invincible. Nowadays they do not believe in miracles.

The whole situation in the Abyssinian camp was cleared up for me by a talk I had with one of the officers of Ras Kassa, Kenjazmatch Zakala, who spoke to me quite frankly about their prospects. Zakala is about fifty years old— he himself does not know his age exactly. He is tall, and has intelligent-looking features and a wonderfully low voice. His grey hair was cut short. Our conversation began in front of his tukul—the Abyssinian chiefs live in the same kind of poor huts as their soldiers. He was wearing the national costume with a shamma thrown over his shoulders, and no signs of a uniform. He commanded 1,500 men who were still nearby, but they had orders to break up and march to the river Setit to join up with Dedjaz Ayelu's men. The commander stood before me, apparently only with difficulty supporting himself, not with a stick as one would have expected, but on one of his slaves who stood at his side. The slave clasped the older man in his arms, clutching tight as one only could clutch a life-less object. It was a strange sight to see the big strong man held upright by his little servant. Behind the chief another servant was carrying his best "rifle", a 12-bore shot-gun, which is really meant for shooting grouse and not Italians. The chief officer had an inferior second-rate rifle and heaven knows how the soldiers must have been equipped.

Kenjazmatch Zakala spoke clearly, and although we were in a state of war, I could not see any signs of it in this man. He had come from the south, leading his soldiers for weeks on end and crossing the Blue Nile twice, which in itself is a superhuman feat during the rainy season. They had to undergo all kinds of hardships and the old man came through it all. Mobilisation, state of war, and battles were natural events to him, and war was his delight.

In his opinion the present war was the hardest test for Abyssinia that God had ever sent.

"Abyssinia has experienced many wars," he said in his rich voice, "and she has never been defeated yet. We hope that the enemy will not win this time either, but the task that we have now is too big. The enemy has aeroplanes, guns, all kinds of explosives, and good wireless communication, while we have nothing of that kind of thing. How can one disable aeroplanes with mere sabres? How can one fight against poison gas with spears? Our people are the best soldiers in the world, but they are powerless against miracle-machines!"

"What will happen in this war, Kenjazmatch?" I asked him. I was used to hear in answer to this question that there was no doubt of Abyssinia winning, although I knew that the people did not believe it in their hearts, but Kenjazmatch Zakala was speaking frankly.

"I cannot yet say. It is possible that we in our own country which we know, will keep the upper hand, but if the Italians are able to hold out on a long campaign, then we have a difficult task. But I do not believe that the Italians could stand a rainy season in Abyssinia. War must cease during that time. They will have to camp here and will be left entirely on their own, for communication of any kind will be ruled out. If we can drag on till the next rainy season, we can bring the war to a victorious end."

Then he began to question me, asking how many inhabitants there were in Italy and was stunned when I told him forty millions. He then asked me how many inhabitants there were in his own country, and when I said ten millions he became cross.

"Just think," he said later, "how are ten millions going to conquer forty millions. It is quite impossible!"

He had no idea of the world outside. He knew nothing of the existence of the League of Nations, and that the Abyssinian question was being dealt with before the League. I told him about the machinery of the League of Nations, but he remained sceptical.

"I do not think," he said, "that the ferentshis (foreigners) will achieve anything. The war will be waged here and not at the League of Nations."

He had only a vague notion of Europe and the Europeans. He thought that Europe was a country like Abyssinia where, just as in Abyssinia, various tribes lived. He knew three of these tribes, the "Inglis," the English, the "Francia," the French, and the "Sherman," the Germans. He knew of no other nations, and for example had no idea that the white officer with Ras Kassa was a Swiss. As far as he was concerned, this man was a "Sherman," and the Belgian with the Crown Prince a "Francia." He suspected England, he hated the French and did not know what to make of the Germans.

"I think that they are our friends," he remarked after much consideration.

I pressed him to explain his opinion of the English. After hesitating for some time, he pointed at his mouth and said, "Malefianu," after that he pointed to the region of his stomach, saying "Kuvu." I did not understand what he meant. But later on I found out the meaning of this explanation. He wished to infer that though the English

spoke kindly to the Abyssinians they really were greedy for
the country. At another occasion I got more samples of
his peculiar figurative language.

I spoke to him at length on the real value of the Abyssinian generals. He himself was not very much convinced
of their ability, but that did not seem to worry him much.

"We have," he said, "three generals who may be able
to defeat the Italians. One is Ras Amama, the second Ras
Tairara and the third Ras Mabil." I knew Ras Desta,
Ras Kassa, Ras Sugonm, but had never heard of the three
he mentioned. Smiling Zakala explained: "Tairara means
mountains, Mabil means food, and Amama means diseases. These are our allies in this war."

The Abyssinian methods of warfare during this war
were even more primitive than those in Europe at the time
of the Thirty Years' War or even during the Crusades. A
Belgian military expert told me at the time that the whole
Abyssinian munition supplies would only last for a few
days, if it should come to modern fighting.

But the average Abyssinian did not worry about that,
for they all relied on their old fashioned weapons; on their
curved sabres and spears which were tipped with snake-
poison. They even felt anxious about their "large" supplies, for they only paid up their thalers for such purposes
with regret. Even at that time every Abyssinian had to
contribute one thaler for the rifles and bullets supplied by
Belgium. Their exchequer is always empty. I was told this
by the Finance Minister who explained that they had in
all twelve thalers. For regular taxes are unknown in the
country, and if they are levied, a "bad impression" is
made. The customs duties are the only national income
and the greater part of these find their way into the officials'
pockets while the rest are the Emperor's only source of
income. So it was that the Emperor, who was the only

man in his country who foresaw how necessary it would be for the soldiers to have modern equipment if success was to be achieved, had to pay for this rearmament out of his own funds. He finances the whole war on the Abyssinian side. The cost is not exorbitant, for the upkeep of Abyssinian soldiers is comparatively cheap.

Nor have the soldiers themselves changed any more than their weapons. The Emperor decreed last year on April 11th in his speech to Parliament that every soldier had to wear uniform, but this order was not strictly obeyed. Now and again one did meet soldiers turned out in a khaki tunic or khaki trousers, but I was never able to find one fitted with a complete uniform. Only the commanding officers who had enough money to pay for their own kit, had new uniforms cut for the "great war," and they had them tailored to their own design out of the cheapest Japanese khaki. Even then they threw over their splendid garb the national garment, the shamma, a kind of toga which matched the ensemble well enough as it is usually dirty enough to pass as khaki.

Most of the soldiers, however, wore their usual civil clothes, a form of dress that is very unpractical in battle for its white colour shows up at a distance and the shamma handicaps movement. But the natives cannot be persuaded to dispense with them in line of battle and even have a special method of wearing them while fighting.

In Cilga 2,500 soldiers were mustered, but only 500 had rifles. These privileged ones belonged to the troops who had been specially selected and some possessed 7.9 Mauser rifles and twenty to thirty rounds of ammunition. They were the crack shots and one can be sure that this valuable ammunition would not be shot off to no purpose. Their bullets were to hold the passes and each man shot on his own at Italian scouts or any Italians soldier who appeared by himself in the narrow valleys. These snipers were clever at concealment, and even if the attackers sensed the direction of the shot, they could never discover the position of the sniper.

The rest of these rifle-owning Cilga troops had old rifles and little or no ammunition. As for the others, they had only sabres and spears and any desire that they may have had to possess a rifle was only the typical longing of every Abyssinian who feels a lord as soon as he owns a rifle. These Abyssinians have always lived in an atmosphere of war and during feasts they shot regularly more of their own people than are killed in a skirmish against an enemy. For such people war is part of life.

The larger units of the army also possessed machine-guns, but had orders only to fire them in extreme circumstances, for they had mighty few rounds of ammunition and no hope of getting any more once they had fired off their supplies. Should the war last long their costly new light Belgian and Czecho-Slovakian machine-guns would rust unused. Most of these machine-guns were of the most modern type, air-cooled, and easy to use and to transport. There were, too, a few Abyssinians who could use them to good purpose, but of course, there were no such things as machine-gun squads. Units of 2,000 men were equipped with one, or at most, with two machine-guns.

The army as a whole made a rather pitiable impression and since Adowa fell there was little sign of enthusiasm. They all looked slightly apathetic, specially as there has been so much talk of Abyssinian heroism. Most of the men lay around with nothing to do, but they were ready at any time to march as far as you liked and they were unconditionally prepared to go into war with courage and determination. But somehow genuine conviction was lacking. I could not help feeling that. However, they were easily stirred up if they were given tetsh, a kind of honey wine that is drunk in quantities there. They become drunk very easily and then there is no holding them back. Their leaders know this and accordingly banned the export of honey to the Sudan. They need it for the enthusiasm of their men.

The white clothes of the soldiers are filthy and they look under-fed and ill.

In Shinda, where I met Dedjaz Ayelu's troops, I saw still worse examples of the contrasts that are to be seen in this so-called war. The Balambaras, an officer who corresponds approximately to our rank of captain, received me to show me over parts of the camp. He was "equipped for war," in that he had a revolver and telescope. Both of these things made him proud. When I befriended him later—and over tetsh we even became fast friends—it was divulged that he could not shoot with the revolver and could not see with the telescope. Both were broken. My companion, Mr. Nauss, mended the revolver and telescope and thereby won his way to the heart of the Balambaras for ever. As a matter of fact, the poor fellow only had four bullets and he hoped to wage war with them.

At some other place we discovered a telephone line. It looked rather strange—it was only barbed wire, but we were assured this was a real telephone wire; they had to use barbed wire otherwise it would have been stolen. The line was modernly constructed and everything seemed to be in order. It had been laid during the rainy season under great difficulties, so that the commanding officers might keep in contact with their outlying troops. Everything seemed all right as long as we did not want to telephone. Telephoning was impossible, firstly because the receiver was broken and secondly there were no batteries for the apparatus. Mr. Nauss repaired the receiver and with the help of all the lamp batteries in our possession, we brought the instrument to life, but it was still impossible to converse, as no one answered at the other end of the line. No doubt they had the same trouble as we, but no Nauss.

I discovered a wireless transmitter in a box at an Abyssinian chief's. He had only just received it from Addis Ababa. The apparatus was in pieces which lay muddled together in the box, and some of the parts were broken. It was a sorry sight to see what had happened to this expensive mechanism. I heard that the chief could not make the set work and thought that it might be out of order. He let an Abyssinian come and tinker with it for three days. Finally this man explained that he was excellent at taking down radio sets, but that he could not assemble them. Addis Ababa surely had to wait a long time before news came from that part of the country.

Apart from these negative incidents, I was not able to discover any form of news service in this part of Abyssinia. I was always told that the troops had the field telephone and radio apparatus, but curiously enough I never was able to trace any sign of these things with the troops I stayed with.

Another thing that seemed extraordinary to me was that the Abyssinians had not heard of maps. Most of the army came from the south and only knew the land from hearsay. A map would have proved useful if they could have read it. One evening as we sat with the commanding officer over a glass of tetsh and the despatch bearers came in with news of the movements of the troops and the Italian advance, I fetched my map and asked the officer to show me the places on it. He took the sheet as a five-year-old child picks up a newspaper: he did not understand a word and all the colours, numbers and other markings meant nothing to him, and I might just as well have shown him a map of South America, for it would have meant just as little to him.

In a few skirmishes the Abyssinians captured a large number of Italian rifles and machine-guns as well as small mountain guns and a considerable amount of ammunition. The rifles and guns were distributed at once among the participants, but they saw nothing of the munition, for that is given out only before battle, but even then the supplies are so small that the Abyssinians must shoot well if they are going to fight a skirmish to a finish without running short of ammunition. The Italian rifles, first-class carbines with detachable bayonets, do not impress the Abyssinians much, for by their standards they are too small. The Abyssinians also say that the Italians of Adowa in 1896 were greater heroes because they carried great rifles. Those of to-day were all young men who came with toy rifles. Most of the Abyssinians who fought in this war were carrying the rifles that their fathers captured at Adowa nearly forty years ago, and they did not want to change these ancient and useless weapons for the neat rifles of the Italians of to-day.

The Abyssinian army was really not an attacking force, its purpose was to defend. It had been ordered not to shoot unnecessarily and this had been done not only with an eye on the munition shortage but also so as not to produce an unnecessarily warlike spirit among the troops. The organisation of this defensive force was terribly primitive, that had not changed with the times and had not been improved with the help of modern war technique. The handful of white officers who were added to the native commanders, could only advise on strategics, and had no influence on the morale of the troops. Their best side was the way huge bodies of men were moved about. In these sphere the organisation worked excellently, but it must be remembered that this was not a very difficult feat for the officers, as the men's commissariat presented only small problems. They wandered daily from one well to another, driving before them the animals which they were to eat later. In the evening the oxen and goats were roasted, cut up and distributed among the soldiers. Ten men were given a leg of an ox to satisfy them, as well as a handful of peas and intsherd (bread), and that was enough. They had no need to consider the transport of other material, as the Italians had to because they had nothing to transport.

The Italians had an efficient and well organised army, perhaps the best of all time because it was the first to be developed entirely in light of the inventions in the armament trade that have been made since the Great War. Three kinds of soldiers were fighting in the Italian ranks. The Blackshirts composed the main army; secondly there came the native troops and finally the regulars. The temper of the Italian army's mettle had not been tested, but the excellent morale of the young soldiers, that is to say the Blackshirts, made a very good impression. These men had been called up out of civil life, whether they worked in offices, or, as was more often the case, were unemployed. They had only given up their Sundays to soldiering, when officers of the regular army initiated them into the mysteries of elementary war-science. With the outbreak of war, their play was turned into the real thing and they became valuable man-power. Foreign military experts who have been watching events in Africa told me that they were most pleasantly surprised not only by the young men's determination, but also by their unpretentiousness.

On the other hand the regulars were not taking such an active interest in the war and tended to sneer at the Fascists' enthusiasm, for these more experienced men have not been steeped so much in the spirit of Fascism,

ITALIAN ANTI-AIRCRAFT GUN—AGAINST WHAT?

WOUNDED BELGIAN OFFICER AFTER BOMBING OF DESSIE

belonging as they do to the pre-Fascist generation. There was, however, no fear of revolt, for the white troops outnumber the black easily, and for this reason the native Askaris' desire for rebellion was not so sharp. The youthful army of Blackshirts was marvel number one in this peculiar war.

The tanks were marvel number two. They, too, were not able to prove their mettle in actual battle, but it was amply clear that they could cope with the difficult country. When I returned after seven weeks from the North Abyssinian bush, I seized on the newspapers that I had missed so much while I was away, and found pictures of tanks attacking Adowa. These pictures were certainly fakes, as Adowa was captured without tanks and without fighting. But before hostilities broke out no military expert would have believed that tanks could cover such rough ground as they were now doing every day.

They can travel at over twenty miles an hour and there is no longer any doubt about their potential performance even in the heat of battle. These tanks had an interesting part to play when the army advanced. They formed a mobile fortress for the troops and before the infantry advanced the tanks moved into reversed arrowhead formation which protected them on three sides, leaving them open in the front only. The column then advanced in this fortified formation. By this method advance guards were rendered unnecessary and the danger of a flank or rear attack was obviated.

The soldiers gave a display of great heroism by day and the tanks put it to good purpose. The heat reached 120 degrees Fahrenheit in the shade, and the steel plates of the tanks made the atmosphere inside intolerable. But the crews grinned and bore it, for they were proving to the world that the Blackshirts are both determined and brave.

Marvel number three were the roads which the Italians built in Abyssinia.   Such roads have never been seen in the country, although the roads built by the Emperor Menelik and Emperor Haile Selassie were considerably more expensive to build.   Since the time of the Romans, the Italians have been renowned as masters of the art of road-making, but until to-day no one would have credited the Italians with being able to build roads successfully over the almost unbelievably difficult mountainous country in Abyssinia.   But here again the Italians have disappointed the sceptics.

They have their own methods.   Their roads do not twist and turn, but are cut straight through rocky country and in this way the road is specially firm and in the end is finished in shorter time.   The engineers in charge of the work were, of course, Italians, but the labourers were enticed from Egypt, the Sudan, Yemen and Syria to Eritrea with promises of high pay.   When they arrived they were treated without the slightest consideration; their wages were not paid, and they were more poorly housed and fed than they would have been in prison.   Work started with the first rays of the sun at six a.m. but the workmen did not get breakfast till ten.   This meal consisted of a can of black coffee and some unrecognisable stuff which the Italians stated to be bread.   Then they worked on till three p.m., when they were provided with a midday meal that was not only bad but meagre and with that in their stomachs they had to last out till sunset.   The evening meal again consisted of coffee and bread with the addition of a little macaroni.   All the work was done in this one fourteen-hour shift and it was only natural for the foreign workmen to feel discontented, and this dissatisfaction was irritated with the additional grudge that they had not been paid for months.   This meant a great deal to these men for in most cases their families at home were starving, and they had only taken their present job to provide them with a little money. When they were disillusioned they tried to escape. Many of them crossed into the Sudan and spread tales of horror about conditions in Eritrea and stirrred up strong anti-Italian feeling.

The 2,000 Italian workmen employed constructing the dam at Jebel Ayula in the Sudan south of Khartoum, contrasted significantly with their prototypes in Eritrea. They did not dream of turning patriotic and migrating to Eritrea to help on the work of their countrymen. I spoke with one of these men at Khartoum. "I am pure Italian," he told me, "but I cannot afford to go to Eritrea. I send what I earn here to my family, for I have a wife and three children at home and they need money. In Eritrea I would not earn anything and even if I did, I would not be able to send it to my family, for it is illegal to send money out of Eritrea."

The road-building in Abyssinia was reminiscent of the creation of the pyramids, not only on account of the huge scale on which the work was done, but also because of the terrible conditions.

The fourth marvel was the airplanes. It was evident that Italy exaggerated the value of her air force and even the military authorities informed Rome that "a war cannot be waged with airplanes alone, to say nothing of winning it." To the perspicacious observer it was not important whether the airplanes stood the test themselves. It was their performance that mattered, and soon after the war began it was realised that in the thin air of the Abyssinian highland the machines lost twenty-five per cent. of their power. But to some extent this was compensated for by the resolution of the pilots who covered the most difficult ground and carried out the most wonderful flights whether they had to fly at record heights or very low. At times they had to fly high to surmount the mountains, and sometimes they had to keep as low as sixty feet because the visibility in the bush was extremely poor. And of course what landing places they could use in Abyssinia were rough and ready, and always small, so that every landing and take-off was an achievement. But both man and machine came up to scratch and demonstrated Italy's high standard of efficiency in the air.

The Italo-Abyssinian war has shown something positive, but it is to be regretted that so much of value was wasted on an unproductive game, for it was all more a game than a war in the modern sense of the word: "It is magnificent, but no war."

Just as the war produced marvels, it also had a seamy side, which was given more prominence in European papers than the marvels. Firstly there was sickness. But here again this war sprang surprises. The Italians did not suffer very badly from malaria because before they left Italy they were injected with a secret Italian antitoxin that made them immune from this disease.

They were injected no less than twelve times and that can also be called one of the marvels of this war for the poor soldiers, in addition to these twelve injections, were inoculated against smallpox and typhus with the result that their bodies seemed to be pricked and stung all over. But all the same these diseases were nearly eliminated and the reports of hundreds and thousands of Italian soldiers brought down with malaria are not true. And where malaria has been ruled out, blackwater fever, the most dreaded disease of all, does not arise.

The only illness that disabled the Italians on active service was pneumonia, caused by the extreme change of temperature at night and by day. The temperature rises to 120 and 140 degrees during the day and at night it falls suddenly to fifty or sixty. The Italians were wearing tropical clothes and they were not provided with coats and blankets as the English were on their North Indian campaigns. They got chills very easily which often developed into pneumonia.

The animals suffered in this way just as much as the men. The camels especially caught a very similar disease, for they had been brought to a country to which they were quite unaccustomed. Camels are indeed objects of curiosity in North Abyssinia, and in many of the villages there the natives are seeing them for the first time, now that the Italians have appeared on the scene. But disease or no disease the Italians had to rely on camels for they could not requisition sufficient mules. I once watched an Italian commission in the Sudan buying up thousands of camels. They had a curious method of working which surprised the officers of the Sudan Defence Force who were assisting them. The Italians had a stick with which they measured the height of each camel as it was led up and if the camel's back reached the top of the stick it was bought. Many poor and unsuitable animals were purchased in this way while smaller but sturdier beasts were passed over. The camels could not stand up to the scarce mountain air and only 4,000 of the 10,000 bought by the Italians in the Sudan are left. Sixty per cent. have, in fact, died.

The mules also died off rapidly and hundreds were left dead as the advance went on. This was not due to the climate but simply because they were overworked and too much was expected of these animals—even more than was expected of the men. The Blackshirts could not be blamed if, on a strenuous march of ten miles in the mountains of Abyssinia, they stacked first their rifles, then their whole equipment on the backs of the overladen beasts, and finally mounted themselves. When the mules broke down under their loads they were left behind, baggage and all. The fate of the animals in this war was no better than the soldiers, and it seems that there is still truth in the saying that men can bear much more than beasts.

Another black side to the war was the living conditions. Water supplies presented the greatest problem, and gifts that helped the soldiers during the Great War so much, such as cigarettes and chocolate, were practically unknown. Macaroni was their staple diet and for this reason the Abyssinians talked of the "Macaroni War."

. . . . .

Dabdo! Two months before I would never have dreamed that I would be spending sleepless nights there, lying on my bed with an attack of malaria. The day before I fell ill, I was in high spirits and we had planned to continue on our secret caravan journey to the River Setit early the next morning. Then everything changed. I had a temperature of 106 and lay shivering under Africa's sun. My companion, the efficient Nauss, diagnosed the trouble:

"You have malaria, old chap."

The camels got the surprise of their lives because they were allowed to graze longer than usual, and they were permitted to munch away for several long days as I grew weaker and weaker, ravaged with fever and pestered with quinine which I had to swallow at intervals.

The sympathy of the Abyssinian natives was charming. As soon as they heard that the "ferentshi," the foreigner, was "amama," ill, they came to my sick bed full of understanding for my position, for they themselves, almost without exception, suffer from the disease in October and November, just after the rainy season when the malarial insects take the villages by storm.

THE "BUSU TSHIKI-TSHIK"

These attacks do not last long and I could soon get up, and pay my first formal visit to the shum, the chief of the village. He was a wizened old Amhara who had suffered from malaria so often that he had grown accustomed to his bed and felt abnormal when he chanced to have no fever.

Dabdo is a peaceful village. In its three dozen tukuls live some 150 Abyssinians who did not give a thought to the war. Here I realised that the country has huge reserves of men, for the male population of Dabdo had not been affected by the war as national mobilisation did not apply here and everyone went about his business as usual. That means in this country that they did nothing. The women do all the work, driving the zebus in the morning to the distant pasture places, then nursing their children—in every hut new born children are crying—and finally they have to prepare the coarse food. Then their day is over. The men pass the day in talk, leaning on their rifles which are never loaded and shouting and gesticulating so violently that they often intimidated me when they were speaking of such harmless things as the weather or the crops.

On Sunday, if it be possible, they do less than ever. A box is brought out in front of the shum's hut and the men sit round it on the ground and play an entirely European card game. All the time they played we heard the roar of guns from the direction of the Setit river, but these fellows were not disturbed by that, and if they did become excited, it was only on account of the game.

There was a peaceful atmosphere in Dabdo contrasting with the thunder of the guns which upset me far more than the Abyssinians whose kith and kin were being killed.

I was often amazed at their calm, especially as I was afraid that as soon as the Italo-Abyssinian war became a reality to them, there would be no holding them back. Later on I realised that this calm was due to ignorance.

The natives have a wonderfully childish trust. They simply refused to believe any bad news, but when a travelling Abyssinian merchant brought good news, they lived on that for weeks.

It was spread abroad in Dabdo that the Abyssinians had been victorious all along the line. They gave exact details, numbers and dates, and told me, for instance, that the Abyssinians had inflicted a heavy defeat on the Italians in the province of Ogaden and were already seven kilometres into Italian Somaliland. Not six and not eight kilometres but exactly seven! And they really believed it themselves! If I had taken in all that the Abyssinians had told me I should have been able to report great Abyssinian victories and a triumphant march on Asmara. But I had reliable sources of information of my own and on the very day that I was told of the victory in Ogaden, I learned the truth: the Abyssinians had been heavily defeated. I had to keep this information to myself for as long as these men played cards I was out of danger, but even at play they had their rifles at their side, and although I knew that they either had no bullets, or bullets that did not fit, I felt that their arms were symbolical of the fact that the Abyssinian is always ready to fight. And when he fights he forgets everything in his war lust and it is all one to him whether he kills or is killed.

But Dabdo was out of the line of fire and the fighting was still distant.

That Sunday the game of cards went on, and the thunder of the guns never ceased; the sun shone fiercely and I lay weak with fever. In the midst of this vapid atmosphere a noise that had never been heard in Dabdo filled the air. At first I thought that it was a car and I realised at once that a car could not pass along the narrow caravan tracks. It must be an aeroplane, or even several!

THE "BUSU TSHIKI-TSHIK"

The Abyssinians forgot their game in a twinkling and grew excited in a different way. I saw their excitement for the first time as they waved wildly and shrieked and searched the sky with their keen eyes. They already knew about aeroplanes and even if they had never heard an aircraft engine, they knew that this voice from heaven could only come from an aeroplane. They also knew that these 'planes brought death with them and that the fighting that only a few minutes before had been far off had become a thing of imminent danger to them. They prepared for battle in a moment and wanted to fight and conquer the aeroplanes in the air, imagining that they could do it with their own rifles.

The hum of the engines drew nearer and I must confess that for the first time during this journey I had an uncomfortable sensation. It was to be assumed that the Italians would bomb the first settlement that they came to and could not be sure that one of their bombs would not hit me. I had not the slightest intention of dying a hero's death in Dabdo, if only because I would then not be able to write about it.

I had often watched anti-aircraft drill and had brought a gas mask with me. Unfortunately it lay at the very bottom of my bag as I had not wanted to disturb the Abyssinians unnecessarily. I tried to remember what I had learned at the drill and to pass it on to my companions.

Were we going to be bombarded with explosive bombs or gas bombs? That was the problem that demanded our attention that Sunday in Dabdo. And while we were still deliberating the first aeroplane appeared from behind the nearest mountain, a tiny speck in the sky. I could not make out whether it was large or small or really did belong to the Italian Air Force.

The shum's son was the first to discover the 'plane and then there was an exhibition of anti-aircraft manoeuvres— à la Abyssinian. I once read that the Emperor had issued new regulations for air attacks, but these decrees were apparently only for Addis Ababa. Dabdo at any rate, knew nothing of the necessary precautions and the same applies to all the other villages. The shum, who had forgotten for the moment all about his malaria and other troubles, suddenly rose head and shoulders above the rest, and feeling that he was the captain of a sinking ship, had the trumpet sounded. It was the one and only trumpet which had been repaired only a few days previously. It had given forth no sound since it had been brought to Dabdo some years earlier. The men who had been scattered about either in their huts or in some other part of the village, appeared before the shum's tukul and where, a minute before there had been no target for a bomber, a group collected in a few minutes which included all the 150 inhabitants of the village. The aeroplanes' work had been made easy and economical, for a single well-aimed bomb would have been sufficient to blow up the whole community of Dabdo.

There appeared a second and a third aeroplane. They were flying very high and suddenly I began to think that they were not taking the slightest notice of Dabdo. I felt that the danger was over, but all the same I felt it my duty to explain to the people how they ought to act when attacked. I begged them to take refuge in the bush, with supplies of water and sand in the event of a gas attack and cloths which they could hold to their mouths to lessen the effects of the poison gas.

All my pleas and commands were disregarded. The group would not break up, and the men, forgetting in the heat of the moment that they had no bullets, aimed their rifles in the air.

In the meantime, the aeroplanes flew quickly by and were impolite enough to drop neither explosive nor gas bombs. I learned later that the aeroplanes were only scouting out the land behind the river Setit to see how many reserves Dedjaz Ayelu who was positioned behind the Setit with his troops, still possessed. Later on the 'planes dropped a few bombs in the bush near Setit to set the withered grass on fire. This grass had been impeding the Italian advance for weeks, and although the Abyssinians usually burn the grass themselves, they now had no intention of doing so, in order to leave it an obstacle for the Italians. In North Abyssinia the Italian aeroplanes had only bombed a few settlings as they could not find anything else in the bush. Reports soon came through to Italian headquarters that the observers in the aeroplanes were in great difficulty because they could simply see nothing. Their only targets were the villages, and they could not pick out the troops in the bush and tall grass. For this reason they were destroying the grass and everything that was hiding in the grass, whether it was soldiers, snakes, hyenas or antelopes.

Dabdo is surrounded and lost to view by the so-called nigger millet, and the tall stalks of this grain camouflaged the tiny village from the flyers. But for the Abyssinians peace was a thing of the past and the community which had wanted to know nothing of war fifteen minutes earlier, in the face of the roar of guns and alarming war news, was suddenly seized by a violent war fever. Even if the aeroplanes caused no visible damage in Dabdo, they made our position thoroughly uncomfortable.

It was a long time before the Abyssinians returned to their cards. I tried to take matters into my own hands and arranged a little anti-aircraft practice, but as soon as they were back at their cards they forgot not only all about the aeroplanes but also my instructions.

This small and, I grant you, negative episode, gave me an insight into the Abyssinians' idea of aircraft and their so-called passive resistance against air attacks.

Only a few hundred thousand Abyssinians had any conception of what steps to take during an air attack. Millions took no precautions when aeroplanes approached and they even lightened the bombers' task by their childish lack of foresight, and the protective measures were weakest in the places where the danger was greatest.

Otherwise Abyssinia was very active in the air. The Italians were not the only 'planes in the sky, for the eight aeroplanes of Abyssinia were always busy, but they were only fulfilling the duties of messengers. For months the Abyssinian pilots had practised nothing but dropping letters and picking up messages from the ground, and they had acquired such skill that the Emperor was enabled to send orders and other despatches to his commanders and get their replies.

.   .   .   .   .

The enemy force was versed in all the cunning of modern warfare and had brought all their most deadly apparatus to Africa. The Italians could not use their highly developed organisations. Their aeroplanes indeed proved worthless at first for the frightening of harmless Danakil natives is hardly a purpose big enough for a military aeroplane. These poor savages had never seen aeroplanes in their lives and could not distinguish between a bomber and an act of God. Poison gas could not be used either, for it sinks down from the mountains into the valleys and the Abyssinians were always stationed high up and the Italians were usually in the valleys. And of course, instruments which signal and ward off air attacks were of no possible use here because there were no enemy aeroplanes. The enemy was primitive and so the Italians were forced to employ primitive means of attack.

Between 1897 and 1898 a French company approached Emperor Menelik of Abyssinia. They wanted to buy a concession for building a railway between the port of French Somaliland, Jibuti, and the growing capital of the Ethiopian Empire, Addis Ababa. Menelik was fresh back from his impressive victory at Adowa and as he already saw the possibility of Italian "revanche," he only granted the concession unwillingly, for a railway in a country which has no roads and whose greatest security is its inapproachability, has a special strategic significance. Although he finally gave in, he reserved the right of deciding the route himself, when the track was laid. This decision surprised and disappointed the French, for he decreed that the line should run via the Hawash mountains and then through the Danakil desert. The Emperor knew that a railway that ran through the desert would lose any strategic significance and the desert of Danakil is a part of the world that the Creator must have fashioned when he was in a bad mood. There is neither water nor vegetation, and the sand extends indefinitely, only relieved here and there by volcanic rocks. Monotony, and relentless heat, that is all to be seen in the desert of Danakil.

Some thirty years after Menelik had made his decision, I travelled along the line that had been built with so much effort, and this journey was one of the most uninteresting and cheerless that I have ever experienced. The engine grunted along slowly through the desert and although the rails had been laid along the southern extremity of the desert, I saw more than enough of the barrenness of the wilderness. We travelled on without seeing a tree that might offer shade. We met caravans belonging to the luckless tribes who had to cross it, as they took rest in the scorching sun and could hardly carry on for thirst. From the carriage windows I saw the foot of the Tshirtshir Mountains. In this desolate waste live wild, hardened people who are just as wretched as the nature itself which surrounds them. They are Danakil tribes who had already given the Emperor Haile Selassie plenty to worry about, for he had no power to command them and the laws that he made were not obeyed. Sultans are supreme in this desert, the Sultans of Aussa. They emigrated centuries ago with their warriors from Arabia and claimed this desert for themselves as a hunting ground. But they do not hunt animals; they hunt men, and to the present day keep up the most barbarous customs of the world. A Danakil warrior may not marry until he has killed an enemy and has brought home his severed genitals as a trophy of his valour. Fighting has gone on for centuries here and it is impossible to put a stop to it. Victims are put to death by the foulest means and the white men who lose their way in the desert are looked on by these barbarians as the most prized booty of all.

On the third of October last the airmen in Assba received orders to clear the way for the Italian infantry by bombardment, and on the same day the aeroplanes went up.

The Sultan of Aussa mustered his men, who were delighted to experience at last a real war in which blood would flow, and while the Danakil warriors were touching up their spears with poison and sharpening their swords in anticipation of the expected enemy, the Italian advance into the desert began.

After the aeroplanes followed new monsters. The Italians brought in tanks. They were fast machines that could roll through the desert at a speed of thirty-five kilometres an hour, but they soon had to be decommissioned, for the heat which rose to 120 degrees, made it impossible for the men to remain inside the steel bodies of the tanks. The water supplies soon gave out and although the tanks could travel at thirty-five kilometres an hour, they were dependent on water, and that was not to be found in the Danakil desert, and the crews of the swift tanks had to wait in the desert with parched throats for supplies which had to be brought from Aden and Port Sudan. The men were almost overcome with weariness and heat and on the second day of the advance they heard that the Italian staff's plan was not going to be carried out easily.

It was part of this plan to reach the fortress of Dessie. At first this plan had seemed possible. The desert apparently offered no difficulties to tanks and infantry, for the highest point lay only 600 feet above sea level, and mountains are first reached just before Dessie.

The Italians counted on being able to reach the River Awash very quickly and according to the descriptions of two agents who reconnoitred the country some years before, water always flowed over its bed, all the year round, but this river is typical of all desert streams. Its source is in the southern mountains of Abyssinia and it flows eastwards towards the Red Sea, but as soon as it reaches the Danakil desert, its flow becomes weaker and weaker until suddenly coming as far as the Red Sea, it dries up in the desert.

The Italians were worn out on the second day of the advance and it was to this unreliable water supply that they turned. The sun and the endless desert wore them down and after the successes of the first day when they took Mount Mussa Ali by storm, they advanced more and more slowly, until, just like the River Awash, they stopped short in the desert. The wretched Italian soldiers, who had been so incited to march to victory, stood nonplussed, and their objective was no longer Dessie and its fortress, but only a gulp of fresh water, or a tree which could afford them some shade, or even a green patch to relieve the deadly monotony of the march.

The advance was delayed. Time was lost with the result that the Abyssinians arrived at the River Awash before the Italians. The former had an easier time of it, for coming from Ogaden they were able to march along the river valley and had a constant water supply.

Fierce battles took place, the first and only battles in the Danakil desert, but the sand drank the human blood thirstily. The fresh Abyssinian army adopted the old and proved tactics, the right wing attacking, while the left surrounded the Italians. It was no mean task for the Italians to break through this ring, but they had to if they wanted to save themselves. Many fell on the field during these battles. The Abyssinians freed the desert and the advance on Dessie failed.

.   .   .   .   .

In the midst of glorious green, a landscape that is always luxuriant, is situated the blue Lake Tana, in majestic loneliness. High mountains keep watch over it and woods of papyrus hide it from the eyes of unwanted visitors. A proud race of men live on its swampy shores and in the villages impressive buildings, palaces and ancient fortified castles tower above the rough huts of the inhabitants of to-day.

This blue inland sea is the cradle of Abyssinian culture. Not far from here the kings of Tigre and Amhara fought and fell in the heat of battle. Adventurous Portuguese crusaders and the fanatical dervishes of the Sudan migrated to Lake Tana, but in spite of them it remained Abyssinian.

The Blue Nile has its source in the waters of Lake Tana and for this reason the lake is considered to be the most important reservoir in Africa and it is generally thought that the country which keeps Lake Tana within its frontiers, holds the key position of the Sudan and Egypt.

This lake which is the object of so much discussion, lies 5,756 feet above sea level; it has an area of 1,200 square miles and the deepest parts are 200 feet. On its islands live Abyssinian monks who, in tumbled-down monasteries, keep charge of the holy books of the Church. These tomes are said to be 4,000 years old but in reality they are only about six or eight hundred. They narrate unreliable stories of the origin of the Abyssinian people. The Blue Nile arises at the most southern point of the lake, and when it begins to flow it is called the Abai. This river flows in a huge curve through 500 miles of Abyssinian territory until it reaches the Sudanese frontier. Its flow in Abyssinian territory cannot be calculated with accuracy for it runs through a canyon three or four thousand feet deep that cannot be penetrated.

Two large tributaries, the Dabus and Dadessa, join the main stream before it leaves Abyssinia, and both of these rivers are more important sources of the Blue Nile than the lake itself. The lake supplies only 13 per cent. of the whole stream, while these two rivers contribute 75 per cent., the rest flowing in from tributaries in the Sudan.

Though it is thus obvious, it will surprise many that even if England had complete possession of Lake Tana she would by no means control the sources of the Blue Nile. Before it would be possible to talk of control, the Nile valley in Abyssinia as well as the valleys of the Dadessa and the Dabus would have to be owned and that means the whole of Western Abyssinia, including the agriculturally important province of Gojjam, the wealthiest part of Abyssinia as it has gold and platinum mines at Wollega and rich coffee plantations in the Gore district.

And it is not only the Blue Nile which gets its waters from Abyssinia. . . . The White Nile's principal source is the River Sobat, which rises in Abyssinia and the rainy seasons supply most of its water.

The sphere of English interest stretches considerably further south than is generally imagined, and England demonstrated her lack of interest in Lake Tana by looking on without protest when an American company was granted a concession by Abyssinia to build a dam in the lake. This company finished all the preliminaries long ago and the plan should be put into operation shortly. In the meantime England has built a mighty dam south of Khartoum.

English interests in Abyssinia are sufficiently protected. Her interests were already ensured in 1902 with the erection of an English station on the River Baro, at Gambeila, 100 miles within the Abyssinian frontier. This English station is protected by the Government of the Sudan and is in the middle of rather less than a square mile of land which Abyssinia made over by treaty to the Sudan. Gambeila, of purely commercial interest to England, provides a terminus for her Nile steamers, enabling them to travel on the Sobat and Baro rivers during five months of the year.

Now all the export trade of western Abyssinia, coffee, honey, and wax, leaves the country via Gambeila, and is transported by the steamers of the Sudanese railways to Khartoum, which is the principal market for those products just as Jibuti is the centre for goods from eastern Abyssinia. In time a few roads were constructed here and these are also controlled by English firms, and the gold and platinum mines of Wollega are financed by England, at a loss, for the production capabilities of the mines is doubtful. In some parts, however, prospectors find gold in quantities, especially alluvial gold that is washed in the River Birbir and in the Baro above Gambeila. But these mines are scarcely worth a war.

The Gambeila station is, of course, a hundred per cent. English, and is run by a District Commissioner, who has at his disposal thirty Askaris from the Sudan Defence Force. Captain Maurice, the District Commissioner, has been eight years at Gambeila, and is extremely popular not only with his own people, but also with the Abyssinians. His remark about the Abyssinians is famous throughout the Sudan: "The Abyssinians have been Christians since the third century B.C."

In Gore, the capital of the province of Wollega, there is an English consulate in charge of Captain Erskine and with that the English interests in Abyssinia are exhausted. The Italian Press intentionally misrepresented this station and the few English-controlled concerns and made out that England had vital interests at stake that would be threatened by an Italian invasion. As a matter of fact, England has no Imperialistic aims to pursue in Abyssinia, and during the long history of Anglo-Abyssinian relations, there has been only one punitive expedition; that ended at Magdala when Napier defeated King Theodore—Theodore's son, by the way, was eventually brought up by Queen Victoria at Windsor and is buried there.

England had three times as much common frontier with Abyssinia as Italy, and in this part of the world frontiers mean trouble, and if England had wanted to come up against Abyssinia, she could have made better pretexts in the past than Italy has now.

There have been countless invasions of English territory by uncontrollable Abyssinian slave traders. In 1926 the first serious attack was made in Kenya Colony and up till 1929 no less than 140 such attacks were counted.

In March of 1932 Abyssinian slave traders broke across into the Sudan, and in October of the same year some appeared seventy miles within Kenya. That time 100 natives were killed and 7,000 head of cattle stolen.

These skirmishes have never been political; they are only forays by Abyssinian bandits and for this reason England believes that these "frontier incidents" can be pursued by the police. They have indeed always been settled with Addis Ababa through regular diplomatic channels, and the Emperor has investigated the damages and paid compensation, as far as that is possible, to the Sudanese or Kenya authorities. Punishment has always to be meted out on English territory.

.   .   .   .   .

When I returned from Abyssinia after my second visit, I had great difficulty in convincing everyone that hardly a shot had been fired since the third of October when the Italo-Abyssinian war officially began. At that time the opposing fronts were 150 miles apart and the gun has yet to be invented that can cover so long a range. I was in Abyssinia on November 8 when Makale was taken and witnessed this Italian victory. It was celebrated as a *victory* and the same evening I heard on my wireless that a "day of victory" was being held in Rome.

This is how Makale was actually taken.

General Santini gave the order to advance with Makale as objective on November 5, after the air patrol had reported that all was clear. The Italians advanced and on the first day their forces of white and black soldiers covered no less than thirty miles, which is a record performance; for in the War the men were expected to cover fifteen to twenty miles in a day, and that in considerably easier circumstances. But the Italians were spurred on with promises of rest, and above all, better food in Makale, for they had been living on bad tinned stuffs, the so-called "scatula", and they were longing for even a mouthful of wholesome food.

Unfortunately for them something happened on November 6 that had never been heard of before in the history of Abyssinia: it rained heavily all day and on the following day, from dawn till dusk. The advance had to halt and the soldiers' appetites had to remain unappeased. On the third day, November 8, the fine weather returned and there was nothing to prevent the Italian troops from pressing on to Makale. The deserter, Ras Gugsa, acted as guide. He was supposed to have reconnoitred the district and his troops were to face the music if the enemy attempted to resist. But there *was* no resistance.

About sixty "War Correspondents" had been brought along with the troops in lorries, and naturally the lorries reached the walls of Makale before the foot soldiers. As soon as they arrived the journalists sent a request to General Santini that they might be allowed to enter the town to buy some chickens, but General Santini recognised the ludicrousness of the position and refused them permission.

"First my soldiers—and then the Press!" was the message he gave to the journalists' representative. After some delay, Ras Gugsa appeared at 9.15 a.m. with his army, which was clothed in a comic mixture of Abyssinian and Italian uniforms, and the town was entered. The Italian staff could then report that Makale had been taken—and the journalists could buy their chickens. Adowa, Aksum and Adigrat were taken with just as little effort on the part of the Italians.

Victories—nothing but victories were officially reported by the Emperor and by the two Italian Marshals until we figured out, that if we added all the Abyssinian casualties

245

mentioned in the Italian *communiqués*, no population whatsoever would be left in Abyssinia, and according to Abyssinian assertions double the number of soldiers sent to Africa by Signor Mussolini had been killed. At Khartoum a high official with whom I was discussing the latest messages said: "Three more Italian victories—and the Abyssinians will be in Asmara. . . . "

Anyhow—this would have been a war such as Lord Kitchener might have desired.

"War is too unpleasant, Madam"—he once said to Queen Victoria, "except what appears in the papers. That has to be done—to make war popular."

It is Signor Mussolini's greatest success to have been able to make this peculiar war popular in Italy—in the very same year, when he was proposed in the Hungarian Parliament to the Norwegian Storting—for the Nobel Peace Prize.

SUPPLEMENT

(*a*) MAP OF ABYSSINIA
(*b*) THE WAR IN BRIEF
(*c*) SEVEN MONTHS OF WAR
(*d*) THE LEAGUE OF NATIONS AND THE ABYSSINIAN
WAR

SUPPLEMENT

THE WAR IN BRIEF

December 5, 1934: The Wal-Wal incident.

14, 1934: Abyssinia telegraphs to the League Council, protesting against Italy's attack at Wal-Wal.

August 16, 1935: Three-power conference fails.

September 4, 1935: League Council fails to settle dispute.

October 3, 1935: War starts. Italians cross Mareb River and capture Mount Mussa Ali.

6, 1935: Italians capture Adowa.

November 5, 1935: Italians capture Gorahai on southern front.

8, 1935: Italians capture Makale.

18, 1935: Sanctions against Italy.

28, 1935: Marshal Badoglio supersedes Marshal de Bono.

December 6, 1935: Dessie bombed. Emperor escapes injury.

15, 16, 17, 1935: Battle of Takkaze River: Italians' first repulse.

22, 1935: Battle of Addi Abbi: thousand dead.

30, 1935: Mussolini admits the "indispensable pause."

31, 1935: Italian 'planes bomb Swedish Red Cross unit near Dolo: 30 killed, 50 wounded.

January 12, 1936: General Graziani launches southern offensive, eventually reaching Neghelli.

15, 1936: Abyssinian Red Cross depôt, commanded by Major G. A. Burgoyne, at Waldia, bombed. Fourteen killed.

February 15, 1936: Italians capture Amba Aradam in battle of Enderta.

249

ABYSSINIAN STOP PRESS

February 28, 1936: Italians capture Amba Aladji, opening way for advance on Addis Ababa.

March 1, 1936: Ras Kassa's Army smashed in battle of Tembien.

3, 1936: Ras Immiru's Army smashed and in flight.

4, 1936: Italian 'planes bomb British Red Cross at Kworam.

29, 1936: Italians capture Sokota on march south.

April 1, 1936: Battle of Lake Ashangi. Emperor's army guarding road to Addis Ababa wiped out.

13, 1936: Italian forces, under General Starace, reach Lake Tana and Sudan border.

15, 1936: Italians capture Dessie, the Emperor's headquarters.

29, 1936: General Graziani captures Sasa Baneh, breaking the Abyssinian "Hindenburg line."

May 2, 1936: Emperor in flight. He leaves Addis Ababa for Jibuti.

3, 1936: Looting and shooting in Addis Ababa.

5, 1936: Italians six miles from Addis Ababa. Ras Nassibu leaves Abyssinia with Wahib Pasha.

6, 1936: Italians enter Addis Ababa. The war is ended.

SEVEN MONTHS OF WAR

AFTER a remarkable campaign of seven months the Italians reached Addis Ababa from Eritrea, a distance of about 420 miles, with a high-power thrust, in contrast to the thrust from Somaliland.

It was on October 3 that the dust-stained legions of modern Rome poured across the border river of Eritrea, marching into the rugged frontier country of Abyssinia with all the machinery of modern warfare. Behind them toiled armies of labourers constructing roads forward as the fighting men advanced.

SUPPLEMENT

Three days later the Italians acclaimed the wiping out of a stain on the nation's history by marching into the town of Adowa, where an Italian army had been massacred by the Abyssinian hordes in 1896. They had covered twenty miles cautiously and efficiently with very little real fighting. Aeroplanes attacked any enemy band in sight. Soon afterwards the Abyssinian Holy City of Aksum fell.

At the same time the Italians were pressing northwards from Somaliland, and the next success to be announced was the capture of Gorahai, a month after the fall of Adowa.

Still the northern army hastened slowly, and it was not until November 8 that the strategic town of Makale was captured, and Ras Gugsa, the renegade Abyssinian prince, was reinstalled in his palace there by the Italians to whom he had deserted with his followers. It had taken the Italians a full month to cover the sixty miles from the Adowa line to Makale.

The Italians then set about consolidating their grip on Tigré and there came a pause. The Abyssinians now tried to cut the lines of communication between Adowa and Makale, but only succeeded in staging some spectacular raids behind the Italian lines.

Then on November 28 Marshal Badoglio, Italy's greatest soldier, superseded Marshal de Bono in supreme command in East Africa and started to prepare a bolder campaign. He showed the new spirit by sending his bombing 'planes to attack the Emperor's headquarters at Dessie, but the Emperor escaped injury, and world indignation was aroused by damage done by bombs to hospitals and Red Cross units at Dessie.

About a week later came the first big battle of the campaign, when the Abyssinians inflicted the first repulse on the Italians, driving them back from the line of the Takkaze River.

But the Italians drew a breath and came back at the Abyssinians, a battle developing at Addi Abbi in which there were heavy casualties and the Italians reported a victory.

A week later Signor Mussolini announced that the time had been reached for an "indispensable pause."

251

ABYSSINIAN STOP PRESS

So the New Year came with the Italians marking time. Further indignation was aroused in the world by the bombing of the Swedish Red Cross unit on the southern front.

But in the middle of January the Italian southern commander, General Graziani, made a spectacular thrust along the far southern border of Abyssinia, where it marches with Kenya, and reached Neghelli. This was designed to clear his left flank in preparation for a northern thrust against Harar and the Jibuti-Addis Ababa railway.

Another comparatively uneventful month passed and in the middle of February the Italian northern advance, which was to develop into a quick-time march on the Abyssinian capital, began.

Victory after victory was reported by the Italians. Amba Aradam was captured after the battle of Enderta, Amba Alaji, key to Dessie and Addis Ababa, fell into the Italian hands. Then the smashing of two Abyssinian armies was announced. The forces of Ras Kassa, the "Black Fox of Ethiopia," whose elusive tactics had so worried the Italians in an earlier stage of the fighting, were reported to have been smashed in the battle of the Tembien. Two days later the Italians reported that Ras Immiru with another Abyssinian army had been completely routed.

Now the Italians were jubilant, but the world was shocked by the news that war 'planes had bombed the British Red Cross unit at Kworam on two successive days.

On went the Italian push, sixty miles from Makale to Sakota. That was at the end of March and the speed of the advance was increasing.

Then on April 1 came the biggest battle of the campaign. The Emperor massed his men for a last desperate defence of his headquarters at Dessie. But sheer bravery was no match for the war machinery of the Italians. Time after time the Emperor, directing the battle himself, threw his warriors against the Italian lines only to see them mown down by machine-guns and artillery fire.

At last the Emperor's army broke and the Italians had won

the battle of Lake Ashangi. Scores of war 'planes swooped low over the fleeing Abyssinians inflicting heavy casualties upon the terror-stricken warriors.

With no resistance to meet, the Italians pushed on to Dessie rapidly and marched into the former headquarters of the Emperor on April 15. Meanwhile two motorised columns had thrust out towards the north. One reached the shores of Lake Tana, headquarters of the Blue Nile so vital to Egypt, and took occupation of the whole shores of the lake without encountering resistance. Another column captured the Abyssinian border town of Gallabat without any fighting.

Then came a breathing spell, but little time was lost in pushing on from Dessie towards Addis Ababa. Two columns of troops set out from this point towards the end of April with orders to cover the last 150 miles to the Abyssinian capital as quickly as possible. And Addis Ababa was the end of a march of 420 miles from the Eritrean border, accomplished in seven months.

But now the campaign on the Somaliland front was reaching a vital stage. General Graziani had launched his men northwards towards Harar.

He came up against the Abyssinian "Hindenburg line" south of Sassa Baneh and fierce fighting ensued. But the Italians forced their way northwards, coming to close grips with the efficiently trained troops directed by Wahib Pasha, the former Turkish officer who commanded a machine-gun corps at the Dardanelles.

The Abyssinians put up a terrific resistance, holding strongholds and making the Italians fight foot by foot for possession. But at last came the news that Italy had captured Sassa Baneh, and the Italians declared that the way to Harar was open.

THE LEAGUE OF NATIONS AND THE ABYSSINIAN WAR

IN the history of the League of Nations, the War between Italy and Abyssinia will go down as the conflict in which the League first enforced article XVI (the "Sanctions Article") against a nation after first proclaiming Italy to be the aggressor.

As far back as December 14, 1934, Abyssinia telegraphed to the League Council, protesting against Italy's attack at Wal-Wal, in the Ogaden, on December 5. Then on January 3, 1935, Abyssinia addressed an appeal to the Council under Article XI, drawing attention to a "threat of war." On March 17, 1935, Abyssinia asked the Council to examine the dispute under Articles X and XV.

Direction negotiations between Italy and Abyssinia failed and on September 4 the Council started, under Article XV, an attempt to bring about a settlement by conciliation. This attempt also proved unsuccessful and the Council began to draw up a history of the dispute and recommendations for its settlement.

While this effort was in progress the Italian army, without declaring war, crossed the Abyssinian frontier on October 3, 1935, and hostilities began.

Two days later, at a meeting of the League Council, the Abyssinian Government invoked the Sanctions Article.

The Council hastened the completion of its report and recommendations, which were adopted unanimously on October 5. On October 7 a sub-committee set up by the Council came to the conclusion that "the Italian Government has resorted to war in disregard of its covenant under Article XII of the Covenant of the League of Nations." The same day the Council accepted, by a roll-call vote, the report. Two days later the League Assembly signified its acceptance of the report by "silent assent." Fifty nations, members of the League, had agreed that Italy had violated the Covenant and that Sanctions had become applicable.

As a result of this decision sanctions were applied against Italy as follows:

(1) An embargo on the delivery of arms to Italy.

(2) A financial "boycott" of Italy, which prevented all loans for the Italian Government, all banking credits for the

Italian Government, all loans for public bodies, persons or corporations in Italian territory, all banking or other credits and all issues of shares or other appeals for capital.

(3) "Boycott" of Italian exports and embargo on the export of key products to Italy.

In addition there has been the proposal that exports of petrol to Italy, necessary for her Air Force and mechanised forces, should be stopped. This has never been carried beyond the proposal stage. Meanwhile Italy has used her warplanes and mechanised columns with great success. With their aid she has advanced with astonishing swiftness both in the north and in the Ogaden.

During the meeting of the League Council in London a move was initiated to bring about direct peace negotiations between Italy and Abyssinia. This effort failed. Germany's reoccupation of the demilitarised zone on the Rhine and the holding of the French elections had a great influence on the situation and at the League Council's meeting on April 20 the whole question of action in the dispute was shelved until the next meeting of the Council on May 11.

Throughout the League's intervention in the dispute Britain took a vigorous stand in support of collective action by the nations. Mr. Anthony Eden, speaking at the last Council meeting, gave the warning that a failure over the dispute might wreck the League system. He also emphasised the lesson of danger to be learned by the world from Italy's use of poison gas in Abyssinia.